Father McNabb Reader

FATHER McNABB READER

~~~~~

Selections from the Writings of
VINCENT MCNABB, O.P.

EDITED BY

FRANCIS EDWARD NUGENT

P. J. KENEDY & SONS · NEW YORK

Nihil obstat:

JOHN M. A. FEARNS, S.T.D.

Censor Librorum

Imprimatur:

✠ FRANCIS CARDINAL SPELLMAN

Archbishop of New York

New York, July 26, 1954

Library of Congress Catalog Card Number: 54–10068

Copyright 1954 by P. J. Kenedy & Sons

PRINTED IN THE UNITED STATES OF AMERICA

For

FATHER J. H. BEDARD, S.M.,

*and through him
all my
Marist benefactors*

FOREWORD

BY HILARY CARPENTER, O.P.

Provincial of the English Dominican Province

◇ ◇ ◇ ◇

*Lord, thou knowest all things,
thou knowest that I love thee.* John 21:17

◇ ◇ ◇ ◇

KNOWING his end to be drawing near—it was in fact the
day before his death—Fr. Vincent McNabb was concerned to make certain provisions for his funeral. Calling
one of the younger brethren to him, he said to him: "Dear
Father, I may well be dead tomorrow and there is a service I would ask of your charity. I don't want a shaped and
polished coffin such as they usually provide, nor should I
like to have a brass factory-made cross on it nor be labelled with a brass label. I want an ordinary box made of
the same sort of wood as this floor"—and he pointed with
a smile to the common deal floor, uneven and knotted,
which he had swept day by day with his bare hand, a floor
such as had been his only bed for forty years and more.
"You will want some measurements, of course; go and get
a tape and measure me now; leave a bit extra length for
me to stretch and plenty of room for the shoulders. When
I am in the box and have been taken down to the church,
bring away the lid and get out your brushes and black
pigment and paint a cross on it, a good big one. Then you
will want the inscription; I will dictate it to you: 'Ven. et
Adm. R.P.F. Vincentius McNabb, O.P., S.T.M., Natus 8
Iulii 1868, Professus 28 Nov. 1886. Mortuus'—I don't

know the date, probably tomorrow, but anyway, '1943 Londini.' Now after that I want you to put a Greek inscription." He then recited by heart these words:

Κύριε, πάντα σὺ οἶδας, σὺ γινώσκεις ὅτι φιλῶ σε

They are the words of my text: "Lord, thou knowest all things, thou knowest that I love thee." "Then," he continued, "after the *Requiem* and the *Libera*, to Kensal Green. I don't wish to be taken there in a glass-house. Borrow the builder's lorry and let down the sides. Put me on it, and let the two acolytes sit one on either side with their candles. (Don't light the candles; they will only get blown out.) Have the boy with the processional cross with his back to the driver's cab, and let me be driven to Kensal Green like that. Of course, I know what some people will say: 'That's McNabb and his tomfoolery, McNabb and his publicity, showing off.' But it isn't that, my dear Father, it isn't that. All my life I have preached and when I am no longer alive I shall still preach. I shall preach even with my dead body. . . . Now of course I realise that I have a vow of obedience and you will need the Prior's permission to do all this."

In these his last hours Fr. Vincent was meeting death as he had lived his whole life. In the incident which I have related to you we may truly see a summary of his whole approach to his religious and apostolic life. His humour was there and his humanity, his obedience, his zeal for the preaching of the word of God, his deep sincerity and dislike of the sham, and above all as a central theme his profound and burning desire to love and serve our divine Lord. "Do me a last favor, dear Father," he said to the same young priest. "Read to me the Passion of our dear Lord according to St. Mark."

From his early youth he was absorbed in the pursuit of truth and its understanding, for he realised that truth wherever he might find it would help him to a knowledge and deeper understanding of the ultimate and eternal truth which is God himself. As a young Dominican, he told us, he would try with all his power to use the intelligence God had given him, to think. "Think of anything," he would say to us, "but for God's sake think." He did not use that phrase lightly, as so many of us might. He meant literally that our thinking was for God's sake. All his own thought led him to God, and the fruit of his thinking was in every word he spoke or wrote.

But not even the ultimate truth, which is God himself, was for Fr. Vincent something merely to be known. Truth was to be known in order that it might be loved; it is the greater knowledge of God that can best lead to a greater love of God.

As the inevitable outcome of this intense love of God in Fr. Vincent came the scarcely less intense desire in him to bring all men, as far as in him lay, to this same knowledge and so to this same love of God. This love was a burning flame in him; it drove him into the highways and byways seeking souls; whether in the pulpit or in the public park, in the drawing-rooms of the rich or (as he preferred) in the houses of the poor, amongst university professors or working men, with Catholics or with those outside the fold, the truth he loved would be told and his very love of it seemed to show him the way. He was what is called a "popular" speaker, and he was so in every sense of the word except in the modern accepted sense. He was always concerned to speak to the people, and it was his peculiar gift that he could speak intelligibly to people in every walk of life. But it was his method, not his matter, that varied according to the needs and capacity of his hearers. No matter what the audience, it was the truth, God's truth, that he told. He did not fear to speak to children on the profound mysteries of the Faith, nor did the childlikeness that remained with this Master of Theology to the end fail to win their interest or minister to their understanding. A true son of St. Dominic, Fr. Vincent was, like him, above all *Doctor Veritatis*—a Teacher of Truth.

Few priests have made a greater or more lasting impact on this country as a whole during the present century than Fr. Vincent McNabb. He became something of a legend even in his own lifetime. He may have seemed to some to have been given overmuch to paradox, seemed something of a living paradox himself. This was partly because of his own uncompromising sincerity which stood out so forcibly in an age so much committed to what is sham and unreal. But it was still more because he was so well fitted by nature and grace to appreciate and to reflect the supreme paradox of Divine Truth Incarnate, Divine Truth which is not merely a Divine Idea but also a Divine Person, the Word made flesh, the Word which moves both in mind and heart and which, so freely received, must be no less freely given to others.

He was an outstanding product of his family background and upbringing where the deep, consuming faith of the Irish was grafted on a practically-minded and naturally philosophical stock. For him a Dominican vocation was the obvious, one might almost say the inevitable, one. The teaching of St. Thomas Aquinas inspired by the apostolic spirit of St. Dominic was wholly attractive and satisfying to his truth-loving and ardent character. The Order to which he knew himself to be called in his youth, and in which he was to prove himself so shining a light in his later years, is properly called the Order of Preachers, and its motto is the single word *Veritas*—Truth.

In him there was a rocklike and unquestioning faith and an unswerving loyalty to the teaching of the Church. Yet he knew that he must be prepared to give a reason for the faith that was in him, must be prepared to defend that loyalty. He knew too, none better, how the visible things of creation could help make manifest the invisible things of God. It was with this in his mind that he devoted himself to the deep study of philosophy, of theology and of Holy Scripture. Above all he steeped himself in the Gospel till it became alive for him and he found understanding and love of the Word of God in the Incarnation, found too his own divine commission to preach and to teach.

"Lovest thou me more than these?" asked our Lord of St. Peter for the third time. "Lord, thou knowest all things," answered Peter; "thou knowest that I love thee." And our Lord said to him: "Feed my sheep." It was this greater love that gave to St. Dominic the power and fruit that was in his preaching, moved men to call him "another Christ" for the mind and heart of Christ that was in him. It is this greater love alone that guarantees the power and the fruit in the preaching of his sons, the Friars Preachers. And it was certainly the source of that most fruitful apostolate of the great Friar Preacher whose memory we recall today. When he was quoting the Greek text, Fr. Vincent asked the young Father to verify it in the *Codex Sinaiticus,* of which there was a copy in the library. "That early text will help to confirm my opinion that St. Peter did not say 'Thou knowest *that* I love thee' but 'Thou knowest *if* I love thee.' I am at the end of a long life and even now I do not know if I have loved our Lord as I

ought." But, after our Lord's reply, Peter could have had
no doubt, for he was given the commission to feed the
flock of the Good Shepherd, a commission given only to
those who have that greater love. And that same commission was given so surely and so fruitfully to Fr. Vincent.

Why are we concerned to keep his memory green?
There are those who believe that Fr. Vincent was a saint.
We, his brethren, who knew him so intimately, though we
would not by one word seem to arrogate to ourselves what
is in the sole judgment of the Church, we saw in him at
any rate this intense love of our Lord and of souls. We
knew the almost unbelievable austerities of his daily life,
his love of his brethren; we knew his personal humility,
we whose feet he had kissed when he thought he had
offended us, or worse still for us, when we had done him
some hurt. In this learned Master of Theology and powerful preacher there was the simplicity of a child. While he
was already a dying man prayers were asked for him from
the Rosary Guild. They offered their Holy Communions,
said rosaries, made visits to the Blessed Sacrament, and all
these were inscribed upon parchment in the form of a
Spiritual Bouquet. The Father concerned with the making
of this looked for Fr. Vincent and found him in the library. "I have brought you a Spiritual Bouquet from the
Rosary Guild, Father," he said. Fr. Vincent came to him,
with that wonderful smile, knelt at his feet and received
the offering in his outstretched hands, while the tears of
gratitude coursed down his lined face.

So many of us already owe him so much. We can best
repay our debt by ensuring, in whatever way we can, that
the good he wrought is not interred with his bones. There
is only one other thing he himself would ask of us, as he
so often asked in his lifetime, that we should pray for his

soul. And we, who trust that the Lord he loved has taken him into the eternal happiness of heaven, nevertheless will make that prayer for him. May his great soul, and the souls of all the faithful departed, through the mercy of God rest in peace. Amen.

(*Originally a eulogy delivered on the occasion of the tenth anniversary of Father McNabb's death.*)

CONTENTS

〰〰〰〰

INTRODUCTION

THE PRESENT ANTHOLOGY of essays, conferences, and verse
by that extraordinary priest, Father Vincent McNabb, is
in a sense autobiographical. For so very personal and
candid is Father Vincent's style that it betrays very much
of the man behind the pen. That it does so is doubtless a
very happy thing, for, if Chesterton's appraisal of him as
"almost the greatest man of our time" be correct, it is
surely worth our while to make his acquaintance.

Father Vincent was born Joseph McNabb on July 8,
1868, at Portaferry, County Down, Ireland, and received
his early education at St. Malachy's College in Belfast. In
1885 he became a novice in the English Dominican Province, and took the name Vincent. Ordained priest in 1891,
he continued his studies at the University of Louvain.
Nearly his entire ministry of fifty-two eventful years was
spent in England (he once remarked that he loved Ireland as a mother and England as a wife) where he was at
one time or another—and sometimes all at once—preacher
and poet, lecturer and writer, religious superior and street-
corner apologist. His honors included that of chevalier of
the Order of the Crown of Belgium, and the coveted
Dominican degree of Master of Sacred Theology. Death
caught up with him in London on June 17, 1943.

Death did not come, however, before Father Vincent
had become something of a legend, and certainly one of
the most widely known priests in the English-speaking
world. He profoundly impressed some of the most cele-

1

brated men in England, and uncounted numbers of the quite uncelebrated. Hilaire Belloc was able to write of him: "The greatness of his character, of his learning, his experience and above all his judgment, was something altogether separate from the world about him. Those who knew him marvelled increasingly at every aspect of that personality. But the most remarkable aspect of all was the character of holiness. . . . I have known, felt, and seen holiness in person."

Belloc's sentiment would doubtless be echoed by many who knew or had come into contact with Father Vincent. The hundreds of "Babylondoners" who met the lean old man trudging their pavements in his billowing habit, or who heard him speak to the crowds at Hyde Park; the thousands all over the world who read the writings, so many of them written while kneeling, which poured from his facile pen; those fortunate enough to have heard him preach, or better far, to have made retreats under his direction; all who revered him for his efforts in behalf of the war-stricken, the reunion of Christendom, the Jews, the poor and the victims of economic oppression; the hundreds who were the personal beneficiaries of his love and compassion; all these would surely speak only high things of that man of whom the Archbishop of Southwark affirmed, "He did good even by his eccentricities."

Many, too, would remember the keen humor with which he delighted his audiences. Whether it took form in pun—he said he carried a McNabbsack and that Ethiopia's capital was Addis-McNabba—or in the jocularity that got people to sing with him the supposed Siamese national anthem, "O WA TA NA SIAM"—"Oh, what an ass I am," it invariably cheered them. But that wit could be incisive, as when at a meeting where eugenic sterilization had been advocated, he rose to say: "You have been advocating the sterilisation of moral degenerates. *I* am a moral expert and I certify *you* as moral degenerates." The preacher at his funeral could justly eulogize him as "God's Happy Warrior."

Father McNabb's social views won him international renown—or notoriety, depending on the viewpoint. He was a great critic of modern industrial life and mass production. Machinery he believed was "taking suicides to Monte Carlo and coals to Newcastle, and all normal human purpose and intelligence to Bedlam." His love for the poor was ever with him. "Often," he said, "when in the eyes of the suffering sons and daughters of men I have seen no tears, I have looked up and seen them in the eyes of Christ." Recalling how Jericho's walls tumbled down when the Jews marched in procession around them with the ark of the covenant, he wrote that if the statue of the Blessed Mother were "carried about the borough of Kensal often enough the slums would fall down." "Back to the land" was a favorite cry of his, property distribution and craftsmanship were causes to which he gave his heart and tongue and pen.

Another cause to which Father Vincent gave unstinting service was that of Reunion. Between 1902 and 1936 he wrote and spoke on this question many times. "God knows," he wrote, "how much I have striven and prayed to mend the shattered unity of Christendom; but never at the cost of shattering the unity of Faith, and therefore of Christ."

As a writer Father McNabb has produced essays that are models of literary craftsmanship; such are to be found in his collection *The Wayside.* His *Oxford Conferences on Faith and Prayer* are carefully wrought as well as theologically notable. The essays on Thompson and Chesterton included in this book testify to the author's penetration and insight. The retreat conferences, of course, can hardly be expected to reveal that polish with which the litterateur will invest his output, but an occasional flashing epigram or deft turn of phrase may be noted amid those urgently exhortatory paragraphs. In any event, I think it true that Father Vincent was not primarily interested in stylistic niceties. He wanted his writings understood and applied, and not merely admired.

The selections I have included in the pages that follow are, I think, representative of Father Vincent's published work. They draw upon an output of close to forty books, several pamphlets, and several hundred articles and verses. It is hoped that they may serve to stimulate further reading in the works of Father McNabb, and at the same time to give the reader at least a glimpse into the great heart and remarkable personality of the man who wrote them.

It remains only to express my indebtedness and gratitude to the publishers who so graciously made available to me material to which they hold the rights, and who are credited at the end of the book. They have all been extremely kind. I would especially mention the Newman Press, Westminster, Maryland, Burns Oates & Washbourne Ltd., London, and the Catholic Truth Society of London. Father Illtud Evans, O.P., of Blackfriars has my thanks for being so accommodating, as have Mr. A. F. L. Deeson of Blackfriars Publications and Mr. Wilfred Preuss of the B. Herder Book Company. To the venerable and gracious Mr. Patrick McNabb, Father Vincent's brother, and to Mrs. John Kiley, Father Vincent's niece, both of Melrose, Massachusetts, go my sincerest thanks for a delightful afternoon in their company. To Sister Mary Eleanor, O.P., Superior of Mount Trinity Academy, Watertown, Massachusetts, and through her to Sister Mary Pauline, O.P., my renewed thanks for assistance beyond my due. To Mr. William J. Lewis for all sorts of co-operation, particularly in the matter of obtaining hard-to-find books, I offer my most heartfelt thanks. To Father E. A. Cerny, S.S., of St. Mary's Seminary at Roland Park, Baltimore, Maryland, for an abundance of patience and good advice, I offer the same. And finally, to my wonderful mother who took the burden of nearly all the typing, I offer, with due sense of inadequacy, my most affectionate gratitude.

FRANCIS EDWARD NUGENT

Baltimore, 21 May, 1954

Essays

A CALL TO CONTEMPLATIVES

THE PRESENT WRITER has had opportunities for observation which few of his contemporaries even in the priesthood have equalled. Drawn from childhood by the dream of helping in the conversion of England, the Master whom he served has led him, during a lifetime, into contact with almost every sphere of Catholic and social activity. It has been his privilege to know most of the foremost Catholics in the country. Many have been his friends, and his teachers. His debt towards them is insolvent bankruptcy.

Gradually, and almost in spite of his youthful convictions, it was borne in upon him that—apart from sin—the main evil in the body politic and ecclesiastic was a displaced centre of gravity. The great industrial town which had naturally fascinated his eyes of youth and dimmed his vision to the land, coming at last into focus, was seen to be not the flower and scent of social life but the scurf and putrescence of decay. Scarcely had industrialism run two hundred years than the great towns were reduced to such a state of economic bankruptcy—and here was the call to an apostle—that race suicide could be made the only practical agenda for the people.

Whilst his conviction was growing from the mere sight of a religious crisis out of an economic crisis, he was increasingly conscious of a verification of his almost unwillingly admitted conviction. For over a century there had been a concentration of ecclesiastical effort in the industrial town rather than in the country. Indeed, there

9

had been something akin to intense cultivation of the
town and something like under-cultivation of the country.
Yet ecclesiastical statistics seemed quite decisive that, in
spite of the numerous growth of people and churches, the
Catholic population of the great industrial town was not
keeping pace with the growth of the population. In contrast with this scanty yield for our intense cultivation of a
rural industrialized people was the fact that Catholic
people on the land could hardly yield anything but a
dogged and devoted Catholic faith. It was not Ireland,
but industrial Ireland that was Protestant; it was not
France, but industrialized France that was free-thinking.
If there was a crisis in the fortunes of the Church it was
because the economic center of gravity had become mis-
placed by a subtle avarice which was endeavouring to
serve God and Mammon.

The call to fulfil our apostolic duty by telling our contemporaries these discomforting facts would have found
us dismayed had not a papal command made sloth high
treason. The Rerum Novarum of Pope Leo XIII had said:
"Every minister of holy religion must bring to the struggle the full energy of his 'mind' and all his powers of
endurance." And the programme demanding this energy
of mind and power of endurance was outlined in these
simple words. "The law therefore should favour ownership and its policy should be to induce as many as possible to become owners."

❖ ❖ ❖ ❖

Thereupon came the great lesson from Exodus, which
after much disjointed thinking finally took this form. "No
people has ever left the town for the land, or remained on
the land when it could have gone to the town, except

under the motive of religion." In other words, by a sheer exercise of economic and ethical induction we had stumbled upon the great principle of Jesus Himself, "Be not solicitous therefore, saying, What shall we eat? or, What shall we drink? or, Wherewith shall we be clothed? For after all these things do the heathens seek. For your Father knoweth that you have need of all these things.

"*Seek ye therefore first the Kingdom of God, and His justice,* and all these things shall be added unto you." [1] And the principle of the Master became all the more moving because it was recorded by that disciple who had quitted the countinghouse to follow Jesus of Nazareth.

◇ ◇ ◇ ◇

This divine confirmation of a truth which we had culled in meditation upon the widowed land of England and the crowded slums of St. Pancras seemed to grow— against our will—into the conviction that all our apostolic work in which we had spent, and intended to spend, our life would be useless without some order of contemplative men going back to the land.

Gradually we seemed to think that what our apostolic thinking had concluded to be a necessity, some of those who loved Church and Motherland might accept as a challenge and a vision. We even went so far as to outline some of the things our apostolic thirst for truth would say to the youths who might be moved by the challenge and the vision. Here are disjointed fragments of our soul.

. . . Seek . . . First the Kingdom of God, and His justice. First things first, for God's sake; or you will crash at once. Let your Exodus be after the coming out of Egypt. Leave the garden cities and the flesh pots, not in

[1] Matt. 6:31–33.

order to scorn suburbia or to lead a simple life, but to worship God.

Quit most of your fellow men not because you hate them or despise them, but because you love them so much as to hate the conditions which degrade and enslave them. Do not leave Babylon as hating the Babylonians, but as hating Babylon, which kills the Babylonians. Leave St. Pancras because you love every one of those thirty thousand families living each in one or two rooms in St. Pancras.

Quit Babylon for love of the Babylonians. And do not seek ease or security you can obtain by using Babylon. What will it avail you to cease living in Babylon if you do not also cease living on Babylon?

If God allows you a plot of soil, and hands for toil, why should you be solicitous to have your revenues from Babylonian brickworks—your meat from Babylonian cold-storage—your drink from Babylonian water-works—your clothes from Babylonian cloth-factories? Is there no clay in Sussex soil—are there no cattle in Sussex meadows—is there no water in Sussex wells—is there no wool on Sussex sheep? Be a monastery then—a MONK—a thing apart, aloof from the world; indeed, be a world apart, a self-sufficient, self-supporting kingdom; and though you surround yourselves, your lands with a high wall of brick and a higher wall of silence, your sermon will be the heart and hope of all the sermons we apostles will preach in the daily exercise of our craft of apostle.

SEEK . . . FIRST . . . HIS JUSTICE

Study not merely to give God His due by worship, but to give man his due by justice. Let not individual poverty beget, as uncurbed it will beget, collective riches. What is superfluous to your poor estate distribute. This is distributive charity; a virtue so sacred that crimes against it are the forerunner of inevitable doom.

Measure your lands by your needs. Measure your needs not by the world's measures, but by the ell or by the King's Arm. Let your standard be not Babylon, or Thebes, or Paris, or New York, or London—but Bethlehem, Nazareth, Capharnaum, Calvary.

Go forth, Christian soul, to the unfallen earth, and there amidst the tares and briars sing the song of work that is worship. Soon around your croft will gather a sheaf of homes and homesteads, where the GREAT SACRAMENT may prepare the ploughman for the furrow, the monk for the choir, the priest for the Altar.

DIEU LE VEUT. FIAT.

(*The Church and the Land*)

THE CHILDREN'S CATECHISM

〰〰〰〰

THE CATHOLIC CHILD—I had almost said, especially the Catholic child in the poor schools—is supposed to have an implicit knowledge of philosophy which is a high compliment to its intelligence. The Catholic Church speaks nobly of children reaching the age of reason. Moreover, with profound insight into human nature, she puts this age not at forty or twenty-one years, but at seven years, when she teaches children their first lesson in freedom by helping them to see and say out (confess) their sins.

Before these little ones are thought fit to make their first declaration of their free will by acknowledging their faults, and therefore their power, they are prepared by a noble handbook of philosophy, fitly called The Children's Catechism. As every country has its own method of writing and arranging this catechism, we take for our present purpose the catechism which, within a stone's throw of where I am now writing, is being taught to children of perhaps the most crowded slumland in the world. In sheer philosophic gratitude let me set down the first eight questions of this appeal made by Alma Mater Ecclesia, dear Mother Church, to the philosophic intelligence of her children of seven!

1. *Who made you?*
    God made me.
2. *Why did God make you?*
    God made me to know Him, love Him and serve

14

Him in this world, and to be happy with Him
forever in the next.

3. *To whose image and likeness did God make you?*
   God made me to His own image and likeness.
4. *Is this likeness to God in your body, or in your soul?*
   This likeness is chiefly in my soul.
5. *How is your soul like to God?*
   My soul is like to God because it is a spirit and is
   immortal.
6. *What do you mean when you say that your soul is
   immortal?*
   When I say that my soul is immortal I mean that
   it can never die.
7. *Of which must you take most care, of your body or
   your soul?*
   I must take most care of my soul; for Christ has
   said, "What doth it profit a man if he gain the
   whole world and suffer the loss of his own soul?"
   (Matt. xvi. 26.)
8. *What must you do to save your soul?*
   To save my soul I must worship God by Faith.

◊ ◊ ◊ ◊

This fragment of literature torn from the front page of
a catechism for the seven-year-old children of the poor is,
for the present writer, a priceless gembook of literature
and philosophy.

In the realm of letters, is there any masterpiece in any
language that opens so dramatically as this, with its almost fierce accost, "Who made you"? If, since the time
of Genesis and Plato, dialogue has been looked upon as a
supreme form of literature, is there any more dramatic
dialogue than this traffic of question and answer between

the wisest institution in the world—and a child of seven?

But even the literary value of this page is less than its value in philosophy. So much sound Greek thought has been assimilated in this Catholic "milk for babes" that these schools of Catholic children, and especially of Catholic poor children,[1] are becoming the last homes of a liberal education. Already in the sixteenth century Giordano Bruno, on seeing the decay of philosophy, which had spread from the reformers, called Oxford "the widow of sound learning." But his wounded philosophic soul would have been soothed if he could have heard the Catholic children of the poor answer their catechism.

Accustomed as I am to philosophic categories and thoughts I should yet despair of enumerating all the philosophical principles to be found implicitly accepted by the child who answers these deep, simple questions.

Especially remarkable is the acceptance of that great Greek generalisation—the Four Causes.

Who made you? (Efficient Cause.)

Why did God make you? (Final Cause.)

To whose image and likeness did God make you? (Formal Exemplar Cause.)

Is this likeness to God in your body? (Material Cause) *or in your soul?* (Formal Internal Cause.)

Now the present writer, who has taught not only children but university students for some thirty-two years, bears psychological witness to the fact that little children even from the poorest classes usually give not a notional, but a real assent to these questions. The men who ask for a simpler creed not infrequently are ignorant of the childmind, and in their ignorance, for something, like a primrose or a toy, which the child can understand but cannot

[1] Who do not necessarily learn typewriting and shorthand.

explain, they substitute something like progress or evolution or ether, which the child-mind can neither explain nor understand!

Notice how deftly that part of philosophy called ethics (Qu. 7) is based upon that part of philosophy called metaphysics (Qu. 1, 2, 3) and psychology (Qu. 4, 5, 6).

Notice again how Descartes' discovery that truth should be investigated sectionally is here made to build up, stone upon stone, an unshakable fortress of truth. Hardly a spear-point of attack could find a fissure between the perfectly fitting courses of the structure. As a synthesis of thought it is masterly. Or again notice that the great truths underlying these questions are all within the discovery of human reason, yet human reason is not merely patient but expectant of faith (Qu. 8).

It will or should be conceded that an institution which offers even its children such solid philosophical food is doing its duty by philosophy.

(*The Catholic Church and Philosophy*)

THE PASSING OF CHILDREN'S GAMES

Now that it has been found necessary to organize societies of grown-up folk, who will in turn organize the games of children, it may be asked whether some great evil is not threatening the commonwealth.

Plato has told us that one of the surest forebodings of a nation's death is any great change in the songs the people sing. He would have been a better prophet of his own people, and Greece, that had begotten a thousand philosophers, might have welcomed one Saviour had he known that an even surer sign of a nation's death is any great change in the games the children play. When "the glory that was Greece" came to the crossways of life and death, the children in the streets of Corinth and Athens were worthy of Plato's eagle eye—had he been philosopher enough to have taken the children not as a toy but as an omen.

In the thirteenth century children left their ride-a-cock-horse and dolls to play at Crusades. Within a century the world saw Notre Dame of Paris, Salisbury Minster, Simon de Montfort, Aquinas and Dante—all of them crusades or crusaders for the defence of some enkindling or waning idea.

It will not be denied, at least by any lovers of sport, that children's games have sickened—it may be to the point of death. Perhaps some of my readers may not understand what I mean by saying that games have ceased to be creative and even initiative. We have largely con-

18

fused games, which children must re-create as they play, with toys, which children merely use to enjoy. The great national games are a dispiriting study in the same ailment. They are now mostly composed of a few skilled players who are paid to play, and tens of thousands of onlookers who pay to be amused. Yet to be amused is passive; not active or creative in form and function. But to "play" bears an active meaning or reminiscence; and reminds us that children who need to be amused, whilst there is grass in the fields and sand by the shore, are the anaemic offspring of a people on the threshold of death.

It is money-making and professionalism that have been the death of children's games. Nowadays as there is a business side to everything, not excepting the Gospel, so there is an opportunity of making money out of the games our children play. I can even imagine that somewhere in the background there is that supreme creation of Mammon, a "Toy Trust." If there is, then its immediate aim is not to amuse children, but to amass wealth; and its final end will be to destroy children, who, in spite of economics *à la* Herod, are the nations' wealth in bullion.

The toys of children, like the clothes of their elders, are at present the prey of fashion. I wish it were more evident that the changes of fashion are nowadays beyond the control of what our grandparents called a "leader of fashion." If there are persons who claim this survival of decayed nobility they are "leaders" who no longer lead, but follow. The real leaders are the tradesfolk, the manufacturers or general dealers, who insist that the next season's fashion in hats or gowns or playthings shall be what they think best, that is, best, not for the buyers, but for the trade. In something less than a generation we have witnessed almost the complete decay of the old games which demanded the fewest toys, and most creative child-like imagination.

My own memories of boyhood are rich in fine games needing not a single apparatus. I still grow enthusiastic over a game we played almost every day during winter. It was nobly called "Wild Boar." Even now I feel my mid-life blood grow suddenly warm as I recall X——, the swift, graceful runner, who could slip through forty or fifty boys all struggling to catch him with an honest boy-ish grip. Yet this manly game needed no bats, no balls, no goal posts, no wickets, no nets. Our only apparatus was daylight, a stretch of open ground, and a pack of boys who could run!

"Follow-my-leader!" Has any toy purveyor ever made a toy worthy to take even a dog's part in this splendid creation of childhood? The very sound and shape of the words belongs to the poetry of life—yea, to the very life of poetry. Even as a metaphor "Follow-my-leader" en-nobles almost every topic that can employ it. But who ever made a noble metaphor of a toy train or a teddy bear or a gollywog?

Another fine game I played, with my elders, when quite a child, in the open spaces of Belfast when I was a firebrand of some five or six years; and I have never heard of it being played since. It, too, was nobly named "Fire-on-the-Mountains," and was a game for the eve-nings and the darkness. I remember that it called into prominence the sturdy daring boys whom with rare in-stinct the rest of us were even proud to follow. It was played fitly at the foot of the sombre heather-crowned mountains that wall Belfast Lough from the winds of the north. "Fire-on-the-Mountains" had been probably played on the shores of the splendid Lough from the days long before history, when the coast of Ireland was kept by an unbroken line of "forths," whence beacons flashed the news of an enemy's approach. That the pirate island never yielded to Roman or Norseman invasion was, I sometimes think, due to the children's game, "Fire-on-the-Mountains," which even now stirs within the breast of mid-life the fierce fellowship of a boy.

There are a thousand reasons for this unnerving decay of children's games. After the spread of money-making and professionalism, perhaps the chief reason is the decay of children. When a home holds but one or two children at the most, toys, playthings, and organized games become a domestic necessity. The child-boy or child-girl lacks that best of playthings, namely, two or three brothers or sisters. The noble art of child-play is entrusted to a paid nurse, whose apparatus is the bought toy and plaything. The child is amused, as precious pet dogs are taken out on a lead to be exercised. The tragedy of decaying child-play may be written in six acts.

◇ ◇ ◇ ◇

Act I.—Horatio Dives, the only begotten son of John Dives (née Murphy) and Marian Dives (née Tomkins), has no elder or younger brothers to play with or fight with.

Act II.—A nursery is set up in the abode of Horatio Dives, where, under pretext of "bringing him up," the said Horatio is imprisoned for the term of his natural boyhood. Several jailers (alias head-nurse and under-nurse and nursemaids) are paid to see that Horatio does not live like an ordinary boy with five or six ordinary brothers and sisters.

Act III.—The head-jailer (alias head-nurse), to pacify

Horatio in his struggles for his birthright of boyhood and freedom, discovers the efficacy of teddy bears, gollywogs, and that kind of thing.

Act IV.—Mr. Makepenny, the sweater and multiple storekeeper, discovers money in teddy bears, gollywogs, and that kind of thing. He thereupon develops the "toy-line" of business. The motor cars outside his Piccadilly and Fifth Avenue stores congest the traffic.

Act V.—All the lesser people, to whom the moneyed classes are the Communion of Saints, buy toys for rapidly decreasing families.

Act VI.—! ! ! (*Curtain*)

Dead March in *Herod.*

(*The Wayside*)

RIGHTS OF THE PARENT

In these moments when the State, which only succeeds in "muddling through" its own task of civil government, is preparing to take over the still harder task of bringing up families, it is the duty of Catholics to realize the rights of parents.

1. *The Rights of the Parent are Natural Rights.* Our English language does not bring out the full force of the Latin words *natura, naturalis,* which are here used. It is almost a pity that we cannot literally translate the more accurate Latin by saying "The rights of the parent are birthrights." In saying that we mean that these rights are not statutory rights depending on man's will, but they are natural rights depending on man's nature (*natura,* or birth). By this we do not deny that these rights may come into existence in any individual case, and thus may be occasioned, by man's act. Thus marriage, which is the remote occasion, and procreation, which is the proximate occasion of these rights, are confessedly the acts of man. But according to the teaching of Catholic theologians these acts are obligatory on the human race, not indeed as individuals, but as a race.

THE WILL OF GOD

When, therefore, a child is born its parents find themselves possessed of certain rights which, though occasioned by their own acts of marriage and procreation, are

23

not determined by their own will, nor by the will of the State, nor by the will of man, but by the will of God.

2. *The Rights of the Parent are prior to the Rights of the State.* This is clearly seen by those who recognize the Catholic doctrine that the family as a family is prior to the State. Not only in idea but in fact, families must have preceded States. The primitive political organization presupposes a group of primitive families. Indeed, the very idea which lies at the root of a State, and all the political arts which make States possible, are borrowed from the natural organization of the family. The wedded union of two hearts that beget a third is no gift or doing of the State's. It is older than any commonwealth. It would still live if all commonwealths came to death.

It is truer to say that the State has duties towards the family than that families have duties towards the State. A nation's chief duty towards this living and essential thing is to safeguard it. But they that watch over it must never sleep, and never overstrain their powers of defence. It is such a sacred thing, so delicately shapen and framed by God, that even its defenders must not lay thoughtless hands upon it lest, like the over-willing defenders of the Ark, they be struck dead.

Thus the home, with its dowry of natural rights, is an older institution than any law of Parliament of men.

A GREAT PRINCIPLE

3. *The Rights of the Parent are the Best Safeguard of the Rights of the Child.* This principle is one which psychology guarantees as an idea and history witnesses to as a fact.

Thoughtless folk whose vision has been darkened by meddlesome philanthropy can hardly be expected to see that even in idea childhood could have no better guardian than parenthood. These people are often heard to ask "why we hear so much about the rights of parents, and so little about the rights of children." Their foolish question shows them ignorant of the psychological principle that although the rights of parent and child seem to be two, these two are really one. Until the child is of an age to defend itself against those who merely seek to use it, or improve it as a means to an end, the child's rights are centred in the parent, the only one whom nature has empowered to love it as an end in itself. No other institution in the world either loves the child as the parent loves it, or even loves it at all.

Indeed, far greater and more unselfish than the love which provides nine-tenths of the matter of our fiction is the love which is rarely dramatized. The romance of two souls who take themselves for better or worse is hardly more than a symbol for that extraordinary love which springs up between the parent and the child. Indeed, in the history of mankind the most marvellous deeds have been wrought by the breadwinner for his babe in his home, or by the mother for the suckling at her breast.

PARENTS' LOVE

It will be said that many parents are unfit for their task or even disloyal to their duties. Many, I agree, in the aggregate; but few in proportion to the millions of parents in the world. Indeed, the devoted love of even modern parents to their children is probably the vastest social force in the world. Although a violent crusade against parenthood has now been troubling humanity for a century, the devotion of parents as parents has no rival except the devotion of men and women as children of God.

DANGEROUS LEGISLATION

For the thousandth time we must warn Catholics against benevolent legislation which seeks "the life of the child," only to accomplish its death. We do not accuse these legislators of being evil by design, because we do not know whether the evil they work is wrought by malice or ignorance. We only know that whereas malice is always the greater crime, ignorance may often be the greatest danger. Moreover, we are reminded of the never-to-be-forgotten words of his Eminence Cardinal Bourne: "Legislation under the guise of Social Reform tended to mark off all wage earners as a definitely servile class. While the Constitution had increasingly taken on democratic forms, the reality underlying these forms had become increasingly plutocratic." It would ill become the Catholics of these countries to be found once more asleep; especially in the important matter of the rights of the parent, which are the divine and therefore the most efficient safeguard of the rights of the child.

(*The Church and the Land*)

NAZARETH MEASURES

AN OPEN LETTER TO THE NEXT
PRIME MINISTER

As your identity is still, while I write, unknown both to yourself and to me, I shall have no misgivings about the pain my words may give. It is not as a politician, but as a priest, I offer you some of the official wisdom learned from my masters. In other words, I humbly offer you in your day of power the gathered wisdom of a class, who, whilst holding aloof from the politics of the City of Man, have yet given their blessing and counsel to every historic city men have built.

If your will is even level with your power you may be able to add a few courses in the building up of the England that is to be. Yet, unless your eyes have hitherto been held, you will have learned that stone upon a stone does not make a wall; nor wall joined to wall, a city.

THE BUILDER

more than any other craftsman, needs the level, the plummet, the square. Every stone he sets must be in its place under pain of endangering even the stones already set. He who would raise a city, a house, or even a wall, must be humble enough to true the work of his hand ten thousand times in the working.

Here may I call your mind from Whitehall to Greenwich—from the business of Whitehall to the significance of Greenwich? At Whitehall there is a throng of men, legislators and administrators, and a still denser throng of

27

clerks to the legislators and administrators. All these men are engaged in scanning England, and Englishmen.

At Greenwich there is a small group of men who scan the stars!

Yet without Greenwich what and where would Whitehall be? The ship of the State would be without helm or chart if Whitehall alone were the guide. But the little group of men who scan the skies, and keep

A THOUSAND VIGILS

in their love of the stars are the seers without whose wisdom the ship of the State would be helpless in the trough of the seas. Few men are given gold for their services more stintedly than these scholars whose eyelids are "gold-dusty" through living with the stars. Yet if gold were the authentic reward of service these men would be the millionaires of our modern civilization. It is not you of Whitehall, not even you, the Collegium Pontificum of Downing Street, who control. It is these "starry amorists," whose star-standards of length and weight and heat and force and time measure the very garments we wear and the hours at which our legislators foregather to deliberate.

◇ ◇ ◇ ◇

From Greenwich learn the significance of Nazareth. Jerusalem was a metropolis as London is a metropolis. Nazareth was a village as, compared with London, Greenwich is a village. But Nazareth, like Greenwich, is the place where all the Sovereign Measures are verified and kept.

GREENWICH TIME

measures our day. Nazareth Time is the measure even of eternity. All our personal and social building, to be lasting, must be trued by the measures of that little school of Seers whose names are the very music of life—Jesus, Mary, Joseph!

Most humbly, then, do I beseech your wisdom, if not your power, to pilgrim ever and anon to Nazareth lest you be found to have builded in vain. The time-measure of Nazareth is nothing less than Eternity; and the Master of the Measures none other than the Ancient of Days. Therefore in all your lawmaking be what Plato wished all men, and especially all lawmakers, to be: "spectators of all time and all existence." The Home of Nazareth recalls our poet's words: "They dreamed not of a perishable home who thus could build." Moreover, the

NAZARETH MEASURE

of length and weight and worth is the Family—that terrestial "Holy and Undivided Three." Let no guile of social usefulness betray you into hurting the authority of the Father, the chastity of the Mother, the rights and therefore the property of the Child. Social and economic laws are more subtle but not less infallible than physical laws. No programme of good intentions will undo the mischief caused by an interference with family life. As well try to arrest a thrown bomb by a plea of good intentions as try to prevent the final ruin of the State by the plea that our ruin of the family was well intentioned. Give no heed to the buyers and sellers who would make Whitehall seek its ultimate measures from Lombard Street and not from Greenwich. England's final doom is not with the trader and his wares, but with the Seer and his stars. And Nazareth, not Jerusalem, is the City of the Measures of God's kingdom on earth.

(*The Church and the Land*)

TO THE CHILD IN THE MANGER

A MONOLOGUE WITH THE SON OF GOD

*"Pray for me, Father. It will be hard for me this week.
I don't suppose I shall do much work this Christmas."*

O ETERNAL SON, O Ancient of Days, these words which
I speak to Thee were first spoken to me, Thy unworthy
priest; and spoken, therefore, to Thee whose priest I am,
though all unworthy. They burned my soul as a searing
iron; because Thy servant who crooned them unto me
beneath his voice was in the full winter of a long, toilsome
life. His grey hairs, his halting limbs, O Deus Fortis, were
crying to Thee for the wage of eternal life. Yet was he in
want even of the wage of temporal life.

O Hidden Paradox of God, who linkest extremes into
Thy unutterable Unity, Thou knowest that when this my
brother, whose years made him as a father, crooned his
mild miserere to me, his father in God, I could have cried
or died for grief at the mystery of his miserere. In Thy all-
seeing, Thou dost know how baffling to my sight and
understanding was this dirge of his, that "Christmas, this
year, would mean no work!" Forgive my blindness of
mind—or was it stubbornness of heart?—that for a moment could not understand how a man should grieve that
Thy coming to the Crib should mean a lull in his daily
round of toil. My soul remembers with joy what Thou
didst say of Thy coming: "Come to Me, all ye that labour
and are burdened, and I will refresh you." O Mystery

hidden from eternity in the bosom of the Father, what great mystery is this, that Thou shouldst come amongst the poor and work-weary to rest and refresh them—and that Thy faithful servant should dread the workless days of rest and refreshment? What mystery is this, that so darkens my counsel as to add a deeper hue even to the blackness of the Cave? Lord, that I may see! Son of David, have mercy on me—that I may see.

Is it for this Thou didst become our baby brother—that we should bemoan Thy birthday as a day of wrath? Are the world's looms weaving a web so rare and fair that Thy stopping them is worthy only of a curse? Is the world's traffic so precious that to delay it even for Thee— and to make merry with Thee—is to beggar man? Is the world's work such a boon that Thou, the Riches of the Father, art as a beggar's rag? Is the world's noise music so sweet that Thou, the Word of God, the Eloquence and Poetry and Beauty of God, canst enter the world only as an interruption?

Son of David, Babe of Bethlehem, Thy servant's un-complaining plaint to me revealed him to me; and Thee to me. Thy love for what Thou makest is so deep that not a blade of grass is reaped uncounted, and not a sparrow falls without Thy grief. The glory that was Jerusalem Thou didst account less than nought, as seeing therein the pride that built it, the covetousness that was its riches and its poverty. Outside "the Iron Gate that leadeth to the City" (Acts 12:10) didst Thou choose to be born, lest by Thy birth Thou shouldst seem to hallow what Thou camest to redeem. The hamlet of reproach, the sheepcote which David the shepherd forsook in the pride of David the king—these were Thy chosen dwelling places: their poverty Thy riches, their lowliness Thy might, their poor

Thy chosen ones, their saints Thy Mother and Thy foster-father.

Such memories of dearth and war now crowd our minds that even to dream of Thee in Thy swaddling clothes must be honey-sweet. How far, alas! have we wandered from the stars and scent of Bethlehem that we should begrudge ourselves a day for remembering Thee.

O Eyes of Christ, look through the narrow doorway of Thy cave upon Thy people who, taking Thy light for darkness and Thy life for death, have strayed into a night where no life is. O Mind of Christ, give our foolishness a little of the wisdom and folly of the Crib and Cross. O Heart of Christ, break not of grief, but strengthen our hearts lest they break not of grief, but of forbidden joy.

Thou Fountain welling up into eternal life, we have drunk wells of our own digging and are sore athirst. We have turned our backs on Thee; and now, O thou who bearest the world upon Thy shoulders, our backs are bowed with the yoke of worse than Egyptian taskmasters. Call us home to Thy hearth, to Thy heart, that Christmas may be again what once it was, a time of mirth when the plough shall lie still in the furrow, the hammer rest on the anvil, and only the tongue and feet of Thy children shall be busy with the song and dance!

◇ ◇ ◇ ◇

And when he drew nigh to the house he heard music and dancing.[1]

(*The Church and the Land*)

[1] Luke 15:25.

meditate thus on political issues is not always wrong: unless, indeed, political economy is not ethical.)

St. Matthew tells us: "Then Herod, privately calling the Wise Men (i.e., the Three Kings), learned diligently of them the time of the star which appeared to them. And sending them into Bethlehem, said: Go and diligently inquire after the Child. And when you have found him, bring me word again, that I also may come and adore him" (Matt. 2:7,8).

Herod's zeal for Infant Welfare was not demonstrably insincere. In asking these three Oriental potentates to investigate matters at Bethlehem and to make a report to him, he was acting up to the very best traditions of his class of welfare workers. Indeed, his evident sympathy with the three kings was, in embryo, a League of Nations, to be skilfully guided, no doubt, by the Big (Three plus One =) Four. The priestly class were wholeheartedly on the side of the king who was building a temple greater than that of Solomon.

All Herod's public utterances, and indeed acts, were housed under great moral principles—Town-planning, the destruction of Slumdom, the moral evils of insanitary surroundings, Child Welfare, National Prosperity, the Crime of Unemployment, International Peace, a League of Nations, the Restoration of Religion.

SATAN'S PLAN

But—it is the special boast and business of the Evil Spirit to deceive even good men. Now, good men or weak men can be deceived only under an appearance of good. Crusades can be engineered, or at least financed, not only by heroes or saints, but by international financiers with little concern for the Cross or the Crucified. So subtle was the plan laid by Satan for the deception, if not of King Herod, at least of the other three kings, and for the destruction of the Child King of the Jews, that an angel had to be sent to foil the skill of hell.

◊ ◊ ◊ ◊

Meanwhile, O Child King, Thou sleepest in Thy Mother's arms whilst the great world that plots Thy death under a thousand good titles lies like a hazelnut in the hollow of Thy hand. Sleep Thy child-sleep, and dream Thy child-dreams, O Babe of God, O God the Babe, lest Golgotha miss its Cross, and men their Redeemer. Thou, Prince of Peace, art scarce alighted on our soil than the sword starts from the scabbard, the blood of babes and the cry of comfortless mothers makes every hearth a place of mourning. Undo the gins and snares set for our feet by our foe and Thine; and if we dare seek a quality so divine as Peace, make our thoughts and hearts as simple as the truth, lest we add to our burden of many sins the crime of seeking evil under a plea of good. Amen.

(The Church and the Land)

A CHAIR OF THE PHILOSOPHY OF HISTORY

〽〽〽〽〽

It was a widow's worm-eaten, tottering chair. And it was set up in a basement in N.W.3. In saying this I have unveiled the mystery lying behind what once I wrote under the title—her title, *Too Much for One*. For that undying story which, thank God, I had the wit to write, had been written post haste after the widow R——, R.I.P., had trudged from her basement to tell me of my mistake in giving her as a Christmas dinner what was "too much for one."

My readers will remember how in that quivering phrase from the bowed, half-blind, four-score year widow I had seen more political and economic wisdom than was being vouchsafed by any university, or avouched by any Government report. Moreover, when I recalled how high finance and big business were based on the horse-leech cry, "It is never enough," I saw, and perhaps said that England's saviour, if ever found, would be found not in a bank or in a manager's office, but in a hut or in a basement.

As I honoured myself and my priestly profession by burying the widow R—— in Kensal Green some twelve months ago, I will set down some of the notes I wrote after having speech with her one afternoon in the half-light of her cave-dwelling.

Today, August 6th, 1927, Widow R—— gave me a complete dramatic Philosophy of History. In other words she showed me the right way of looking at things that happen, and even of things that seem to happen wrong. I knew she knew the right and the wrong way of looking at such things because never in all her life had she been more than a week or two from starvation, and often she had to go without food to give it to her little daughter. Such training in the philosophy of history I call "learning at the bench."

In my time I had read Augustine of Hippo's *The City of God,* wherein that African genius at one stroke created the philosophy of history. I had even dipped into, and indeed swum about in, the *Histoire Universelle* of that greatest (?) of French geniuses, Bossuet. So that I thought myself not unprepared for what I might hear in the basement of N.W.3. Yet I believe the brother Bishops of Hippo and Meaux will understand and pardon me when I now confess that even *The City of God* and the *Histoire Universelle* were not fit preparation for the transcendent philosophy of the poor, unlettered, half-blind widow R——. There! I've said it—whether my readers believe me or not.

Talking, then, to me, or to herself—or was it to God?—she expressed the astonishment of the human mind when things happen to our hurt. A sentence or two and a gesture or two painted a complete picture of the seeming hopelessness flooding the soul at such ill happenings.

Then with a dramatic change in her voice she expressed —better than Hippo or Meaux have expressed—the still greater astonishment the human mind feels afterwards. When all these happenings are seen to have been—her word was "beautifully"—planned I cannot convey the perfect picture this unlettered, half-blind, half-dead widow drew in one or two sentences made living with one or two untaught dramatic gestures.

She named God with a certain stillness and hush of reverence. I think she spoke of everything "fitting in." In listening to her I seemed to hear her words as a quiet *vox humana* against the great organ music of Augustine and Aquinas telling mankind that not one happening of earth or sky, nor yet one stirring of the mind and will of man can fall outside the encircling arms of infinite mercy.

Then this four-score-year child of Mary of Nazareth— this younger sister of "the Chair of Wisdom"—recalled to my mind the lowliness of "Behold the handmaid of the Lord!"; as with bowed head and a sob of self-belittling in her voice she added: "There!—I'm not educated. But I can't help seeing it. How good God is to let me see it."

◊ ◊ ◊ ◊

Yea! woman from the crowd, blessed are the eyes that see what thou in thy half-blindness wert given by God to see; and blessed, indeed, the ears that hear what thou amidst the ceaseless din of a city thoroughfare wert given by God to hear!

For half thy sight and hearing I, whom thou dost reverence for my education, would give all I have heard and learned in the Schools. Thou, O basement-dwelling Mistress of Vision, hast been taught in another School; and by another Master. Thy school was Nazareth—or was it Calvary? Thy Master was the Word made flesh who dwelt with thee under thy roof—yea within thy soul.

(*Blackfriars*, Vol. XII)

THE PLACE OF FEAR

A WISE MAN has set it down as his philosophy of life that the beginning of wisdom is a noble fear—the fear of God. It is even more undeniable that only on a foundation of fear can certain heights of heroism be raised. The true hero, like the true saint, is not a man who lacks fear, but who conquers it. Even his heroism, like all his achievements in life, is a conquest; and that most difficult of all conquests—over himself. Yet his victory does not destroy, but bridles fear; which remains for ever within him a fierce steed champing the bit.

Some natures are almost incapable of fear. They face death without the quivering of a lip, or the loosening of a limb. Where others cower and shrink, they stand and almost exult. On the battlefield they never hesitate, but take their place in the deadliest spot as unconcernedly as they would lead their partner in a dance. On land or sea where there is need of some desperate undertaking, they are amongst the few who are at once ready to take their life gaily in their hands.

Yet their fearlessness, if not a fault, is almost a failing. It is based not on any conquered fear, but on something like a missing sense. Theirs is the fearlessness of little witless children, who, whilst the storm rages, will play and frolic in the alleyways of a ship, when the men of the sea are doubly lashed to their post of duty by hemp and fear. These fearless ones know not what it is for fear to beat down the gates of the heart, and freeze every pulse of blood within the veins. They have never borne in their very bodies, and in spite of their will, a fear which is as real as the pains of a bruise or the heats of a fever.

Others have had their whole life coloured with dread. Every day at its dawning has been an offered, and timidly accepted, battle with death's nearest kinsman, fear. Every day at its close has had to record a battle lost or a battle won. Yet if at the day's close a *Te Deum* is sung, it is with a lowly eye upon the undecided battle of tomorrow; and if no *Te Deum* but a dirge closes the day's defeat, the tears of sorrow are dried by the thought that the victory of tomorrow may wipe away today's betrayal.

Life with its increasing struggle against principalities and powers, and its fateful ethical battles, would be almost unbearable were it not for the lesser victories of the soul. Ethics are the substance of life; and etiquette, the lesser ethics, its sweetness. Yet it sometimes happens that some souls to whom the ethical life is a pitched campaign, have little room for the lesser sweetening victories of etiquette. A battlefield is not the most favourable spot for life's amenities.

In the same way it sometimes happens that life's lesser victories are ungained by the great souls to whom the substance of life is a long, stubborn campaign against themselves. These men are heroes to those who know all, and cowards to those who know but part. But when the soul, in whom fear is native and unsleeping, accepts the lesser challenges of life, the victories won give them a sweetness which is victory's most engaging quality. These men are the flower of heroes—the knights not only *sans peur*, but *sans reproche;* who to the splendid heroism of the battlefield have added the sober heroism of the home and the city gates.

It has been said that as all philosophy is the philosophy of death, so is all fear the fear of death. But it has been better said that all fear should be the fear of sin. For this reason it happens that those often fear death least whose sins should make them fear it most; and those fear it most whose sinlessness of life should rob death of its sting. David wrote a psalm whose essence is the phrase, "My sin is ever against me." The whole psalm might appear to some of us as a singularly craven production; the work of a wretched god-worshipper, whose chief emotion was fear. Had we no historical account of its writer, internal criticism might suppose him to be a miserable fanatic devoid of manliness. Yet the writer was the Shepherd King David, his country's liberator, and one of the most warlike and engaging characters of history. There were very few forces in the world able to cast fear into this warrior heart. Yet he feared God, nobly as a warrior should, with a fear begotten of love.

It is part of the necessary psychology of nations to understand their songs, and still more their psalms and prayers. The careless thinker might easily suppose that the solemn minors of a people's poetry and liturgy betokened a sorrowful and gloomy national characteristic. Almost every national treasury of song is the contradiction of this inexpert psychology. One striking example is the literature of the thirteenth century, which has given us the *Dies Irae.* Another hymn or song of the same century is the *Salve Regina.* What will internal criticism judge when confronted with such tenderness shot with terror, as is found in the stanza?

> To Thee do we cry, poor banished children of Eve;
> To Thee do we send up our sighs, mourning and
>   weeping in this valley of tears.

Yet it is not commonly remembered that this strange blend of sweetness and fear was often a war-song; and a war-song of the men who went with Richard the Lionhearted and St. Louis into the mysterious East against the victorious Mohammedans. It was the song not of cowards, but of heroes. Richard the Lionhearted bewailing his sins that had prevented him from walking the streets of the Holy City, is a noble type of manhood, which the mere name of the hero should prevent us from associating with cowardice.

The beginning of all heroism is then a noble fear of sin. The other fears with which mankind is filled can be curbed and even driven out by this master fear. Hardly any follower of Christ has written so much on fear as has St. Peter, whose weakness was to have been overbold. Most of the philosophy of his fall and resurrection is summed up in his consummate phrase, *"Be not afraid of their fear,* and be not troubled."* He would have us remember that just as a man may believe in faith and love his love, so may he be afraid of fear. He even suggests that the most perilous of all fears is thus to be afraid wrongly of being afraid. *"Non timeo timere"*—"I do not fear to fear"—might almost be the motto of the new Peter.

No man can choose not to fear. He can choose only between two fears—a fear which is the way of death, and a fear which is a hero's gateway through a thousand deaths unto life.

(*The Wayside*)

THE CREATOR CHILD

MEDITATION ON A CHILDREN'S HANDWORK EXHIBITION

ONE of my childhood's joys was to spend long stretches of time dabbling my forearms in a butt of water. All I knew about this occupation was that I liked it. Now that I am an exile from the days of childhood I can look back on the joy I felt, and analyse why I liked it. There was the physical reason, that the cool water was a gentle thing, and soothed the spirit. There was the imaginative reason, that since I could not wade or bathe in the sea, I could at least take a dream-bath in the water-butt; and that as pirate ships were as dead as Captain Marryat, I could chase and capture my own pirate sloops in the miniature Mediterranean nestling under the kitchen window. But there was a mystical reason. I never knew of it until today, when I stood in the Newarke School Hall and saw the things children of the elementary schools of Leicester have made out of plasticine. Then, in face of this art of childhood—or this childhood of art—I knew that my joy in dabbling with water was a supreme emotion begotten in the depths of my soul through mystic communion with one of the world's creative elements.

◊ ◊ ◊ ◊

All my readers, and I myself, can remember the joy we had in handling mud; and even in walking through it. We loved to make it into something. Some stupid people, who know nothing of psychology, think that children like to

44

make themselves dirty. No! but children like to make. As "to make" is an active verb, it demands an object; as "John makes a noise; Jane makes a mistake." Indeed, "to make" can be a very active verb, demanding two objects, as "This water makes wood stone"; or, to speak in transcendental terms, "God made clay men."

Now childhood despises limitations. As primeval clay is not at hand, it awaits rain and mud. I have known children to dabble their hands in the offscouring of a city's grime; and make mud into enchanted castles. I have seen children on the steerage forecastle of an emigrant ship dancing round a plain steel stanchion and making it into a forest tree as they sang "Round about the mulberry bush."

One day, in a fit of wisdom which did not last long, I proposed to the thrifty folk of Leicester that they should make a pond for the Leicester children to wade in. I had an idea that, when no one was looking, I might take off my shoes and stockings and wade in it myself. But primarily I wanted the Leicester children to trample the mud or sand or clay. Every healthy child—especially every healthy male child—glories in trampling mud. I wanted and still want some poet to sing this elemental activity. There are noble verses about Greeks treading the wine press; although this is a little troubling to the temperance advocates. Yet to tread out the wine cluster is of yesterday. Whereas to tread out the mud is the elemental activity that made music on the world's birthday.

◇ ◇ ◇ ◇

Plasticine! It is not a handsome word. It is a business word. Men in search of money made it; children could have made it better, if someone had had genius enough to ask them. But the thing plasticine is a child's delight. It is a clay which is kept soft and workable by being kneaded now and then with a little oil. Some financier, who loved money, as I said, made the word; but I would guarantee that some man or woman who loved children and clay made the thing.

Today I saw it in all the glorious forms of children's doing, within the Newarke Hall. It had to compete with the aristocracy of Seventh Standard High Art on the platform. But to me it was a revelation, and blinded me to all else. I called it the Art of Childhood; and when I had moulded this phrase, I found I could turn it round and call it "the Childhood of Art" with equal satisfaction. Plasticine is nothing, and clay is nothing; but the quick fancy and delicate finger of a child are something. Or, to be quite accurate, plasticine and clay are that formless something that a child can shape into something else, the work of its own hands.

On a table apart I saw these things children had made out of clay. My impressions are so manifold and particoloured that I cannot give them shape. I have seen many collections of art, and endless galleries of paintings. They are, too, often but interminable and countless yards of sameness. But on this one table the children had formed of clay a motley group of endless difference. It was a Noah's Ark; that stroke of child-genius. Almost every eerie or lovable object of a child's fancy had been pressed out of the clay by the heart and hand of a child. Antediluvian mammoth creatures lay wallowing near daffodils. A child's flower-twined sun-bonnet dwelt in peace at the foot of a lighthouse. I saw Alfred the Great, crowned and frowning on the threshold of the Danish camp. There were birds and birds and birds, all of them different. A pigsty I saw was a work of transcendent realism. But indeed every flower blossomed; and every animal was alive. A noble swan raised its neck, arched and expectant against man the foe.

But amidst this bewildering harvest of child-art one creation of childhood stood up as supreme as the sheaf of Joseph the Dreamer. At the table-end there was the figure of the Crucified, a sagged and drooping figure whose thorn-crowned head rested on the bosom; and at His feet, the bowed form of a woman who mourned. A child's heart had remembered this supreme sorrow; a child's delicate fingers had wrought clay into the expression of its remembrance. If anyone, at this Passiontide, can see this THING wrought in plasticine by the hand of a child, and can withhold his tears—may he never again see the face of a child!

◊ ◊ ◊ ◊

The old story tells us that once upon a time God the Creator, having made clay, saw it was good; good in itself, and good to be made into something other than itself. Thereupon God took the clay, as the children have done, and made it into daffodils and geese and swans and roses and rhinoceroses and men. Thus it would almost seem that this God loved clay as children love it; or again, that when these frailest of His handwork take clay into their hands and make it into the strange beings that people their fancy, they are but proving themselves to have been made after God's likeness, in God's most childlike ways.

(*The Wayside*)

A TALE OF TWO CITIES

≈≈≈≈

ANNO DOMINI 1913—New York City. This is the date and place of the first part of the Tale. It is such a horrible tale that I must give the exact circumstances, otherwise my readers may think I have made the tale "all out of my own head." But this would be too exquisite flattery for a head whose chief quality is an instinct for knowing where it can thieve to the best purpose.

Time, 3 P.M. Mrs. Marcella Dives, whose husband broke the meat ring at Porcopolis, is seen in 42nd St.—or is it 39th St.?—shopping.

It is now six months since her first baby's birth. The heir apparent of the Dives millions is a fine boy. To see him is to want to cuddle him. Everyone envies his parents. As Judge Elijah Washington Elbow said to Reuben Yokohama Dives: "Say, Rube. You've been investing in Real Estate this time—sure!" But Mrs. Dives has evidently not the judicial mind of E. W. Elbow. At any rate, the fashionably dressed shoppers of 42nd St.—or is it 39th St.?— see Mrs. Dives and a nurse-woman and—the heir apparent. But the heir apparent is in the arms of the nurse. And in the arms of Mrs. Dives is a DOG!

LONDON CITY

The second part of the Tale is like to the first.

Anno Domini 1924—London, Sunday, 10 A.M. A fine morning even for London. I am tramping from N.W. to

S.W. I see a quietly dressed elderly person pushing a perambulator. My heart leaps up as I think of the innocent babe, after three storm-bound days in the nursery, at last released to the sun and air. I am prepared, as usual, to offer the beggar's alms of a smile to innocence in its perambulator; my theory being that the child by mere existence beggars my thanks, as do the snowdrops and the primroses.

As it is the first perambulator I have seen in my tramp from Hampstead to S. Kensington I am ready to be lavish with my smile. Indeed, I will smile so prodigally as to fill up every valley and wrinkle in my face, as I look upon this fortunate babe—whom a devoted and withal sensible mother is taking out to the tender mercies of the air and sun. I look at the perambulator, and see not my beloved innocence—but TWO PUGS!

BABYLON

To me, this is one tale—one horrible tale—one horrible, ghastly, grizzly nightmare of a beastly tale. But my friend, Professor Codex, says that by all the laws of Higher Criticism it is two tales, even as it is two cities. Yet he also propounds the alternative theory that it may be in essence one city and one tale; and that the city is Babylon, and that the tale is Balaam and Josaphat.

◇ ◇ ◇ ◇

But I know what you, gentle reader, are thinking in your heart. You are condemning Marcella and the nameless Lady of the Pugs. Now I beg of you not to be premature. Remember the golden epigram,

De te fabula narratur.

First of all, may we not be thankful that the Heir Apparent was not where the dog was—on his mother's icy bosom? A nurse's embrace was not the best thing for poor forlorn little Dives. But it was infinitely better than the dog shelter. Give even a dog—even a she-dog—its due. Perhaps Marcella had been brought up and even educated (Lord, save us!) for the matrimonial market where women are taught all the arts (or tricks) for becoming a wife; and none of the secrets of being a mother. Perhaps in her humility Marcella felt fit only to nurse a dog. In that case how wide fall our arrows of indignation.

WHO SHALL CONDEMN?

Again, the Lady of the Pugs! Who are you and I, that we should condemn her?—especially that we should condemn her without a trial. Do we know the tragedy that filled her perambulator with pugs and not with cuddling babes? Alas! Babylon-on-Thames and Babylon-on-Hudson are so merciless to their citizens that many a young man and maiden who feel spurred to the adventure of founding a family are doomed to remain unwed—until they have found a house—or two rooms and the use of a kitchen! A bed-sitting room with a gas-ring is not the bare minimum for a husband and a nursery. But it will do for breeding the smaller kinds of dogs. Moreover, dogs do not, like children, scratch the wallpaper and make loud noises on the floor—to the despair of the landlady.

More and moreover, some women must have something to love and fondle. If, therefore, they have no children of their own, who will blame them if, in secret, they kiss and fondle a litter of pugs? The hard critics who would stone this woman with the pug-perambulator

would stone the poor folk who, unable to buy butter, try
to make the best of margarine. Therefore he that is without sin amongst us let him begin the stone-throwing!

❖ ❖ ❖ ❖

THE VILLAINS OF THE PIECE

Again are not you and I, dear reader, the villains of this
tragedy? Have we no sight beyond the tragic Marcella
and the Lady of the Pugs; into that dark system which
begets Marcellas and Ladies of the Pugs as infallibly as
the mother of this litter begot the litter? The offal of the
city—is it all our neighbour's doing; and not somewhat
ours? Are we not in part our brother's keeper? When we
love the things that freeze the mother's heart and dry her
breasts, can we unabashed blame the dry breast and the
frozen heart? Is Babylon-on-Thames and Babylon-on-
Hudson, for us, the kingdom of heaven on earth?

> Is Jerusalem our City—or Bethlehem?
> Is Sion our mount; or Golgotha?
> Is Mammon our God—or GOD?
> *Ipsi viderimus!*

(*The Church and the Land*)

THE HOME OF SONG

FOUR CYCLES of perfect song should make of Bethlehem a high place of pilgrimage for the feet of poets. There on the hillside, where the sheep still bleat and graze and are led afield by their shepherds, David the shepherd lad found his song. Before he died the King David had written some matchless songs, woven from his repented sin. But not even a purple thread of sin repented is in the web of his Bethlehem songs. The shepherd lad, with a still untainted heart, is nature's high priest, and enters his holy of holies with the waving incense of shepherd psalms. He is the first, and perhaps the foremost, poet of nature.

Some of his poems, written at Jerusalem when Bethlehem was only an unforgettable reproach, are full of love for nature, which, in the saints, is but an engaging replica of their love of God. Like the incomparable *Domine Dominus noster,* though written when the shepherd lad had found a throne, they are nothing less in art than a herdsman's night song in the sheepfolds of Bethlehem. Even across the centuries we have but to read them to see the shepherds keeping their night watches by their little flock. The moon wreathed with stars, the dark shadows cast on the hills across the moonlight, the deep night silences of the valleys bear us, as they bore David the shepherd lad, to thoughts of God in His greatness and of the littleness of man. "What is man that Thou art mindful of Him?"

In all this Bethlehem cycle of songs, chanted by a little

52

nation as it lay hemmed in by powerful foes, there is
nothing of the mere narrowness of nationality. This
strange race of men sings its joys and sorrows, its love and
hate; and its psalms become the songs, not of Jewry, but
of mankind. They are the "voice of praise." And though
a shepherd lad sang many or most of them when he had
his home or his heart in Bethlehem, they have been hallowed as the perfect praise which the priesthood of better
things offers up to its hidden God.

◊ ◊ ◊ ◊

When David's songs were almost forgotten in his own
valley, at dead of night the sky enkindled suddenly into a
conflagration of song. The shepherd angels brought God's
Lamb with many carollings to His earthly fold. For us it
was a welcoming. But who of us shall say what it was for
them? Of a truth it was no *Te Deum* they sang on that
night which robbed Heaven of the newborn Lamb. It was,
perhaps, such songs as shepherds sing who set out to seek
the one lost sheep, more precious than the ninety-nine
safe in the wattle-fold. In spite of the brave *Gloria,* which
alone we have remembered of their singing, the midnight
plainsong may have been but a long *Ave atque Vale* to
Him Who had preferred man's indifference to their flam-
ing love, and the brown earth to all the gold of the skies.
But whatever their singing, it was a shepherd song, sung
across the abyss by the white winged herdsmen of the
eternal hills to the gentle shepherd folk of the hills round
Bethlehem.

◊ ◊ ◊ ◊

Another cycle of most perfect song has found no one
bold enough to be its chronicler. She who wove the seam-

less robe of the "Magnificat" to praise the child she bore within her womb, had another burden of song when her Burden lay in her lap. It is to her child a mother sings her sweetest song; and earth has no song more sweet than what a mother sings, in darkness, to her child. It may even be that the unsurpassed *Canticum Novum*— "New Song"—of Heaven will be some cradlesong which Mary the mother will sing to God the Child.

But enough for poetry to know that Bethlehem once overheard God's Mother singing her cradlesongs. The very stones of Bethlehem are of such holiness that Poetry will doff her sandals from her winged feet, unwarned by any other angel but her own love of perfect song.

◇ ◇ ◇ ◇

"From the mouths of babes and sucklings Thou hast perfected praise."

The great tragedy of the Incarnation had its chorus; and these were, by birthright, angels and children. It was the children who broke into song and took all Jerusalem with them on the crest of their singing when on the back of the ass's colt the Son of David came for his crowning to Jerusalem. These little ones had already earned the right to chorus their King on the day of His glory. A thousand of them had sung a babe-song to Him when Herod's sword went aharvesting in the fields of Bethlehem. This thought is not a fancy, but a fact, recorded alone by Matthew the Publican, in whom angels and children have found a fit gospeller.

◇ ◇ ◇ ◇

Bethlehem is thus the Porta Speciosa—the Beautiful Gate—of the Incarnation; made fairer still with four cycles of consummate song. Poetry might spend an age fruitfully in wandering amongst its beauties. Have we not in these songs of shepherds, angels, the mother and the suckling babes all that poetry may dare to sing— songs of earth and heaven, of life and death; or, again, songs of creation and the Creator, and of love and hate? What more can the poet hope to chant?

Some day, when the Bride of Christ comes into her own, Bethlehem will blossom again as in the days of her singing. Set like a wattle-fold upon its hills, there will be a school, not of prophets, but of poets; and a home for singers. Each poet will day by day, or in the watches of the night, lead sheep afield, or overhear, it may be, amidst the vast eastern silences, some angel song from the coast of heaven, and a thousand little ones will offer up their perfect praise to heaven's sweetest Singer, Who, in the Crib and on the Cross, sang with human lips and to human ears the songs of God.

(*The Wayside*)

Biography

FRANCIS THOMPSON

IN WRITING of Francis Thompson I feel as must have
felt Samuel Johnson when he stood through a day of
pitiless rain in Ottoxeter's market place to make amends
to a dead father. One afternoon Sister Mary Michael of
Saint John and Saint Elizabeth's Hospital came to me in
one of its wards and asked me to see a poor man who
was dying. I asked her, as I was bound to ask, if he was
at death's point—or if he had by name besought me. And,
then, God forgive me, I laid hold of the excuse, valid
in law but discredited in the higher law of love, that I
should be trespassing on another priest's fold and that I
must hurry home to my own flock. That poor man dying
almost unknown was one whom I would have walked
barefoot a hundred miles to see—Francis Thompson. And
I had refused to see him!

To me, therefore, it is no great joy to speak of him. I
am but reopening a wound that should not heal. I am
but scourging myself with public and deserved thongs
for discourtesy, yea, a wrong to him whose very faults
have been of service to my soul.

It was with something like personal gratitude that we
received Everard Meynell's Life of Francis Thompson.
Herein has been set by hands of skill and love all that
may or should be known of the poet, who before he died
gave England and the human soul songs that should
not die. All we would say in praise of the Life is that

it fitly and for ever links the name of Meynell with that of Thompson, to the deep joy of both.

A poet who saw the last forty years of the nineteenth century and the first seven years of the twentieth century had set before his eyes many a theme to sing in songs of deep thanksgiving or deep discontent.

Like so many of the men who move the world by the spoken or the written word, like Savonarola and Lacordaire, the poet was a doctor's son. He was even meant to be himself a doctor, and with that intent was sent first to Ushaw and then to Owen's College. It was the good fortune of the poet who was to be, that Ushaw gave him large leisure, a well-stocked library and that quiet survival of literary education which we are learning to envy. Seven years upon the Durham hills or in the Library were gradually revealing to the intending doctor his true vocation.

His stay of seven years on the threshold of medicine at Owen's College, Manchester, persuaded him finally to give up a career which might bring him wealth only by disloyalty to a vision which now became "the master light of all his seeing." It was not the lecture halls or museums or dissecting rooms of Owen's College that welcomed him; it was the libraries, and the Poet's Corner in the libraries; for the young medical student was content only with the company of his peers.

At last the call of song came so imperatively to him that, leaving his hopes of a livelihood behind him, as Peter left his boat and gear, he went up to London—not London the metropolis of political and famous men, but London the desert; London, where men are almost as countless and as valueless as the sands of the Thebaid —London the beloved Mother of the man of action who courts fame and the man of dreams who seeks only to be unknown.

His abrupt renunciation of Owen's College and a career seems to have been accompanied by what his rare Johnsonian sensitiveness called a fault against his father. It might be allowed us in our ignorance to take refuge in the platitude that no doubt faults were on both sides, and excuses due equally to both. A provincial doctor who has begotten a world-poet has a part to play which gives the excuse beforehand to his failures. And a great poet who is fettered with the gyves of materia medica and physiology must be a saint to be self-controlled.

Whatever may have been the facts of this misunderstanding between two minds moving in two different orbits, the faults, at least on one side, were but virtues in the making, after the manner of those human weaknesses and avenues of humility which Alma Mater Ecclesia absolves nobly by a felix culpa.

It is almost with tears that I say that we and Poetry are the gainers by his remembered fault. An unceasing undertone of grief made the strong music of all he ever sang. His poems were always a strong soul thinking aloud and threading all his thoughts with the purple twice-dyed of repentance. You will bear with me whilst the Poet utters his grief.

> But ah! withal,
> Some hold, some stay,
> O difficult Joy, I pray,
> Some arms of thine,
> Not only, only arms of mine!
> Lest like a weary girl I fall
> From clasping love too high,
> And lacking thine arms, then may
> Most hopeless I

Turn utterly to love of basest rate;
For low they fall whose fall is from the sky.
Yea, who me shall secure
But I, at height grown desperate,
Surcease my wing, and my lost fate
Be dashed from pure
To broken writhings in the shameful slime:
Lower than man, for I dreamed higher,
Thrust down, by how much I aspire,
And damned with drink of immortality?

.   .   .   .

Ah, for a heart less native to high Heaven,
A hooded eye, for jesses and restraint,
Or for a will accipitrine to pursue!

("The Dread of Height")

Now that the poet had decided definitely that song
was his vocation, the Muses gave him a long novitiate,
not by "Genesareth but Thames." Before the solemn woo-
ing closed with full wedlock he, like another seer, had
to serve long years. It gives us such different eyes upon
the city streets to know that this novice of Poetry took
upon himself if not the vow heroic at least the life heroic
of what our forefathers called wilful poverty. He starved.
He went without food, until Brother Ass, his body, never
strong and never cherished, took the seeds of that disease which was to be his death. Often he knew not what
it was to lay his head under any roof but the dull glare
of a London sky. He slept like a vagrant on some friendly
seat on Thames Embankment. He worked almost as a
burden ox, for a bookseller, and bore upon his shoulders
heavy sacks of his beloved books. There is more than
verse and sentiment in these verses of "The Cloud's Swan-
Song":

Of my wild lot I thought; from place to place,
Apollo's song-bowed Scythian, I go on;

Making in all my home, with pliant ways,
But, provident of change, putting forth root in none.

Now, with starved brain, sick body, patience galled
With fardels even to wincing; . . .

He sold newspapers and held horses at Charing Cross.
Once a Rothschild gave him a munificent florin for a
paper and entertained a poet unaware. He became the
Mangan of the streets of London, a self-conscious Mangan
as we may read in his splendid prose poem on Shelley:

> If [Shelley] as has chanced to others—as chanced, for
> example, to Mangan—outcast from home, health and
> hope, with a charred past and a bleared future, an an-
> chorite without detachment, and self-cloistered without
> self-sufficingness, deposed from a world which he had not
> abdicated, pierced with thorns which formed no crown,
> a poet hopeless of the bays, and a martyr hopeless of the
> palm, . . . then might he have cast the gorge at life.
> (Essay on Shelley)

Once he was rescued from starvation and death by a
fellow-outcast to whom he has given an immortal thanks
wreathed in the immortal recollection of his dark night
of the Soul.

At length the time came when the Muse took him
to full wedlock. The story of his first published poem
belongs to the romance of romance—the poetry of poets.
Wilfred Meynell and his wife Alice Meynell were jointly
responsible for a literary monthly, Merry England, that
died after a few years; died as die the saints in an undeniable odour of genius. One day a scrap of soiled paper
was pushed through the letter-box. The writing was of
a fashion long gone out of fashion: clear sloping and
with an almost feminine gracefulness. The eyes that read
the poem were those of a poet, and could at once detect

the authentic mark of poetry. It took some time before
the writer of the poem could be tracked like a fugitive
and drawn not unwillingly into the sacrament of a catholic home. For the poet it was as if at a turn of the hour-
glass midwinter had given way to the full spilth of
summer.

The sad annals of Literature hold no page more golden
than that which tells how Francis Thompson, the news-
seller of Charing Cross, became a child beloved in the
home of the Meynells. The gentle poet—whose verse
Ruskin praised fitly in superlatives—took the new-found
poet to her own. It is almost a sacrilege to praise her for
a lack of literary jealousy: as if her mind, so rich in all
the sanctities of emotion, could take any other revenge
on genius but to love it. For the twenty years that the
poet was to live he never again knew the sting of poverty.
With the same love with which they would have fed
the winter sparrow, the home he now called home gave
a welcome to this lark-throated sparrow amongst the
poets. What other poet was ever so happy in his friends?
God alone gave him his soul; but these friends of his
gave him almost all else. God mated his soul with song:
but they, like another Monica, brought his unborn song
to life. In rescuing a poet from himself they were conscious of no desire save that of loving their neighbour
in poetry as they loved themselves. It was well for the
poet that they loved him as poets should; and well for
them that a poet took their alms of love meekly as knowing that the true thankoffering for love is to use it. They
were but gainers by their gift; for he paid them back
their service fourfold, like Zacheus, in golden verse.

It was seven years before the death of the nineteenth
century that Francis Thompson with his volume of Poems

came suddenly to life. Almost with equal truth might we say that with these poems English Poetry rose from its dying bed. One of the poems in this challenging volume was "To Monica Thought Dying." It was a poem in the writer's strangest manner and strangely significant of the effect of his own published verse on the world of letters. In his undying verse he seemed to put without all the lesser minstrels who make a rout. Then he went within to raise the child to life. These are bold words, but not foolhardy; as one may feel who remembers that this volume of the young poet drew near the deathbed of nineteenth century, with its overweighted cornucopias and its fulness of bread, and sang to it the subtle flute warblings of "Love in Dian's Lap," the dirge "To the Dead Cardinal," and the breathless hurryings of "The Hound of Heaven."

Two years later Sister Songs gave childhood the laurel twined with gossamer of delicate and immortal verse.

Later still, whilst the century had three years to run, the poet closed his furrow with New Poems—which to some of us at least is the poet's deepest message of mysticism and topmost note of song.

He had but ten years more to live. These sad years he lightened with no published verse. He had persuaded himself, by some scruple of genius, that his Muse had fled and that nought remained for him now in life but to await inevitable death.

This conviction that his song was dead found a place in his last book.

"The Hound of Heaven" had, even from the beginning, prophesied of this death. He still wrote prose for the Academy and Athenaeum, but these things were less the unwilled inspiration of a throat aflame with song, than the brave efforts of a toiler to eat his bread in the sweat of his brow.

Coventry Patmore, who had called "The Hound of Heaven" "one of the very few great odes of which the language can boast," had added that "the young poet's prose was ever finer than his poetry and his talk better than both." We are inclined to accept the epigram when we know that whenever a prose criticism by the poet reached the editor for whom he wrote, the whole editorial staff would be summoned to hear Thompson's prose read word for word, as a masterpiece of literature. We are further reminded that true literature has two tables of the law, and the poet two pipes of pan, poetry and prose. His poetry is but the throbbing heart of his prose. His prose is but his poetry that has come down, in a mood of lowliness, from its car of fire to walk on foot. In his poetry Francis Thompson donned the high priestly garments to which God had appointed him by birthright of consummate verse. But in his prose, the man of song laid aside his pontifical singing robes, and clad himself nobly with the homespun of the people amongst whom he loved to dwell.

It may be expected of us to offer some reasons why this swift singer so easily took his place amongst the "bearded counsellors of Poetry." As one of the in-experts of the art we can accredit our opinion only by offering it with extreme diffidence.

The poet's first endowment—a gift of Nature stilled intelligently throughout hours of seeming idleness—was his craftsmanship and mastery of words.

Francis Thompson was a master of words. His vocabulary is as full, almost, as Shakespeare or the Ancren Riwle. Yet Francis Thompson has not merely a vocabulary of his own, but almost a language of his own. He makes words speak, as Paganini made the strings speak and even sing. He is a master craftsman who, before he makes his masterpiece, will make the tools that are to make the masterpiece. When he came up for solitude to London he bore two books in his slender outfit, Blake and Æschylus. Blake gave him that simplicity which broke out here and there through the thickets of his subtle thought into such poems as "Daisy" and "Ex Ore Infantium." Æschylus gave him epithets, and Milton redoubled the gift. To make epithets is of the genius of all poetry. Another homelier way is trodden by the philosopher. It is his craft not to centre wisdom in a mystic word fit only for experience or insight, but to break small the stubborn bread of life. He must sift and shred the ray of pure light into its octave of colours. He must diffuse the lightning flash so as to be seen and studied by untried eyes. He must prepare the altar and the altar's victim for the song of the poet and the sign of the prophet. But the poet by his craft and calling must be an epithet-maker. By the finished use of epithets the poet condenses his thought to a fine arrow-point that sings its way into the mind through the eye and ear of fancy, or he presses and welds the broad thundercloud into a fine quivering lightning flash. I take a verse or two at haphazard out of the marvellous poem, "From the Night of Forebeing."

> And there is light!
> Light flagrant, manifest;
> Light to the zenith, light from pole to pole;
> Light from the East that warmeth to the West,
> And with its puissant goings-forth
> Encroached on the South and on the North;

And with its great approaches does prevail
Upon the sullen fastness of the height,
And summoning its levied power
Crescent and confident through the crescent hour,
Goes down with laughter on the subject vale.
Light flagrant, manifest;
Light to the sentient closeness of the breast,
Light to the secret chambers of the brain!
And thou up-floatest, warm and newly-bathed,
Earth, through delicious air.
And with thine own apparent beauties swathed,
Wringing the waters from thine arborous hair;
That all men's hearts, which do behold and see,
Grow weak with their exceeding much desire,
And turn to thee on fire,
Enamoured with their utter wish of thee,
Anadyomene!

Was it this morning light waking and warming a poor
sleeper by the Thames which kindled "in the secret chambers of his brain" the superb lines:

Giver of spring
And song and every young new thing!
Thou only seest in me, so stripped and bare,
The lyric secret waiting to be born,
The patient term allowed
Before it stretch and flutteringly unfold
Its rumpled webs of amethyst-freaked diaphanous
     gold.

(*ibid.*)

The poet's sudden leap into fame was due less to his
craftsmanship than to his message. Not only the form was
noble poetry but the theme was noble poetry. His action
was as a King on his execution day: "He nothing common
did nor mean Upon that memorable scene."

This "conduit running wine" of purest mysticism recommended him all the more to his contemporaries because agnosticism, which had been a characteristic quintessence of the nineteenth century, had left men's lips parched and cracked for poetry. Thompson has written:

> It seems to us that Shelley was struggling—blindly, weakly, stumblingly but still struggling—towards higher things. His Pantheism is an indication of it. Pantheism is a half-way house and marks ascent or descent according to the direction from which it is approached. Now Shelley came to it from absolute Atheism; therefore in his case it meant rise.
>
> Again his poetry alone would lead us to the same conclusion for we do not believe that a truly corrupted spirit can write consistently ethereal poetry.
>
> ("Essay on Shelley")

Now agnosticism, psychologically speaking, is the offspring of intelligence divorced from Truth and Conscience unacquainted with the Commandment. Agnosticism is logic lacking emotion, and logic is the antipodes of poetry. Therefore as a matter of history agnosticism has always made a good pleader and an indifferent poet; for the reason that it is rhetoric and logic rather than poetry. Between logic and poetry lies the great world of life, over against which the authentic poet sits, a spectator of all time and all existence.

It was the boldness of Francis Thompson in an age of agnosticism and mammon to offer the incense of poetry to the true God. His poetry was as imperative as a Credo. You can hardly understand a line he wrote until you realize to your dismay that his sin is always before him, and he is at pains to lay it before his readers. Yet he knew and almost persuaded the self-elect to admit that his Redeemer liveth. He would not own that his mind was narrowed by admitting the existence of the Infinite. He would not repent in sackcloth and ashes that life had lost its colour because a God of infinite personality and power pursued him with infinite love. He would not foolishly reject the splendid vision of God in man, Heaven on Earth, Infinity in a span, merely because some men with no light in their fancy nor song in their throat denied the thing they could not see, even though it was the desire of their heart and of the eternal hills.

The mission of the poet to an age sickening of agnosticism has often found expression in the poet's own words:

> Suffer me at your leafy feast
> To sit apart, a somewhat alien guest,
> And watch your mirth,
> Unsharing in the liberal laugh of earth;
> Yet with a sympathy
> Begot of wholly sad and half-sweet memory—
> The little sweetness making grief complete.
>   ("From the Night of Forebeing.")

> Only that, 'mid vain vaunt
> Of wisdom ignorant,
> A little kiss upon the feet of Love
> My hasty verse has stayed
> Sometimes a space to plant.
>   ("Retrospect")

You will remember Wordsworth's lines on Contemplation. But they pale beside the supreme mysticism of his younger brother poet.

Here we contrast him almost against our will with Milton and Shelley whom he looked upon as masters of his craft. Milton is one of the first, as Thompson says Shelley is one of the last, of the metaphysical poets. But every proof he gives that Shelley is the last of the meta-

physical poets is its own refutation; they but prove that
the writer is himself a later poet of the same school. It is
easy to group under one title of metaphysical every poet
whose theme is set beyond the physical and natural. If
Francis Thompson deals with the soul, Milton and Shelley
deal with the soul in its unreasonable revolt against the
infinite. Thompson's song is religion; Milton's is theology.
Thompson makes us love Christianity, Milton makes us
detest Calvinism. When we have listened to "The Hound
of Heaven" we pray to pray, we long to believe, we hope
to hope, we would love to love the God who is thus a
pursuing hound and a consuming fire. But when the
sombre fires of "Paradise Lost" are shut down we are almost in love and at least in sympathy with that splendid
rebel with his immortal lines:

"To reign is worth ambition even in Hell. Better to
reign in Hell, than serve in Heaven." Milton's "Paradise
Lost," like Thompson's "Hound of Heaven," sings of a
God who pursues the sinner. But the God-hound of Milton is yearning to devour, whilst the Hound of Heaven
is yearning to embrace the soul whom it pursues. The
hurrying feet that pursue so relentlessly the fleeing soul
of the poet and sinner are the fair feet of Him who cometh
upon the mountains with good tidings of great joy.

> Halts by me that footfall:
> Is my gloom, after all,
> Shade of His hand outstretched caressingly?
> "Ah fondest, blindest, weakest,
> I am He whom thou seekest!
> Thou dravest love from thee, who dravest ME."
>
> ("The Hound of Heaven")

The contrast with Shelley takes us almost further into
the heart and sanctuary of true poetry.

How far is this frame of mind from him who spoke of himself as "unsharing in the liberal laugh of earth"—the *riso del Paradiso* of Dante.

The truth is that Shelley, not being able to brook the bridle of law, Prometheus-like set out to thwart it. He deposed the God of the world; nor would he adore another God than one of his own image and making. Nature which he began by deifying he could end only by defying; until toying with her tresses he is strangled by the pitiless caress of her water nymphs.

On the other hand, the writer of "The Hound of Heaven" looks upon himself through the eyes of God. He sees himself a being divided against himself. He is a physician who meekly confesses that he cannot cure himself and will not practice upon others. His parched lips whence his withered dreams had borrowed meet cere-cloth were soothed in the travail heats of dying by souls cloistered and dedicate to the Hound of Heaven.

Poet of Death, he died in a home of death and in the month of the dead!

All and more than all the strength of Shelley is, by this poet of the sanctities of life, compelled to build a nest for fledgling faith, wan hope and timid love. There is deep reverberation in both the poets' song. But in Shelley's song it is the crash of a world overthrown by man's revolt: in Thompson's it is the thunder of withdrawing waters of chaos or the exultant clamour of a world that for the first time sucks up redeeming blood. When we read the splendours of this "Ode to the Setting Sun" or of any of his marvellous Odes we may say within ourselves perhaps "such things could Shelley have said, had he but seen them." Alas! he could not see them. For Shelley the religion of Nature was but a pagan mythology; for Thompson it was mysticism. Had Shelley been converted to live he would have been as Thompson, for the conversion of a poet is but a going forward from mythology to myticism.

Even when Francis Thompson pillowed his head on the stony pavement, in his withered dreams he saw, like another Jacob, a ladder reaching from Heaven to Charing Cross. Angels made traffic to and fro along his ladder of vision. He had no Promethean anger against Him whose feet the ladder touched and to whose praise the poet's song was sped. He took his own high achievements in song not as from himself but as gifts carried by the trafficking angels to his soul and tongue.

His mysticism is a synthesis of everything in love:—the love of God. But unlike the hybrid mysticism of the salons and drawing rooms it was seated on asceticism.

XIX

Where is the land of Luthany,
Where is the tract of Elenore?
I am bound therefor.

XX

Pierce thy heart to find the key;
With thee take
Only what none else would keep;
Learn to dream when thou dost wake,
Learn to wake when thou dost sleep,
Learn to water joy with tears,
Learn from fears to vanquish fears;
To hope, for thou dar'st not despair,
Exult, for that thou durst not grieve;
Plough thou the rock until it bear;
Know, for thou else couldst not believe;
Lose, that the lost thou may'st receive;

Die, for none other way canst live.
When earth and heaven lay down their veil,
And that apocalypse turns thee pale;
When thy seeing blindeth thee
To what thy fellow-mortals see;
When their sight to thee is sightless;
Their living death; their light, most lightless;
Search no more—
Pass the gates of Luthany, tread the region Elenore.

("The Mistress of Vision")

There was a hidden mystery about his emotions that I know not if we should seek to unveil. Yet what tenderness of emotion is in "Daisy" and "The Poppy." These things which most men make a matter of joy he made merely a matter of renunciation. He is at enmity with no one but himself. He has words, as we have heard, of unutterable sweetness to her who put fire within his heart and a poppy in his hand; and to her whose mercy to his starving lips won mercy for her sin. He is haunted by the memory of his own waywardness, and feels himself hunted always by the Hound of Heaven. But he is not embittered from first to last. In all his verse you will find no sneer—save against those who sneer. He has faith in faith, love for love, disdain only for disdain. He scorns only the scorner.

He is not proud. He has just that frugal self-consciousness which makes a great soul abashed more by the fulness than the failure of its achievements.

As a theologian who deals professedly with the philosophy of the world and of God I am often astounded at the insight of this dreamer into the deep things of God.

There is one incomparably deep thought begotten of Augustine the sinner.

Happiness is the shadow of things past,
Which fools still take for that which is to be!
And not all foolishly:
For all the past, read true, is prophecy,
And all the firsts are hauntings of some Last,
And all the springs are flash-lights of one Spring.
Then leaf, and flower, and fall-less fruit
Shall hang together on the mellowing bough;
And silence shall be Music mute
For her surchargèd heart. Hush thou!
These things are far too sure that thou should'st dream
Thereof, lest they appear as things that seem.

("From the Night of Forebeing")

◇ ◇ ◇ ◇

The true philosopher, says Plato, is one who prepares
to die. It was the keen realisation of death that arrased
the poet's song with purple like a house of kings. He
had written haunting verse.

Her song said that no springing
Paradise but evermore
Hangeth on a singing
That has chords of weeping,
And that sings the after-sleeping
To souls that wake too sore.
"But woe the singer, woe!"—she said; "beyond
the dead his singing-lore,
And its art of sweet and sore
He learns in Elenore!"

("The Mistress of Vision")

Ten days before his death he came to the Hospital of
Saint John and Saint Elizabeth served by the Sisters of
Mercy. It was noticed that the frail body was almost
fleshless and was no weightier than a child's. He would
not be served by the lay nurses; yet in the hands of the

Sisters he was as obedient as a child might be. All day long he lay upon his back motionless. The Sisters told me that they noticed how his eyes were always gazing upwards. They added, "We never saw such a brow—such a brow!"

From time to time when they bent over him they could hear him murmur—and his murmurings were unintelligible to them. "My withered dreams! My withered dreams!" At dawn on November 13, 1907, he passed for judgment before Him whom alone He sang in all the unsullied sweetness and strength of his song.

The same love that gave him a home in life, gave him a home in death and raised over his grave the stone that can but symbolize, until it perish, his imperishable name.

(*Francis Thompson & Other Essays*)

ST. DOMINIC

On Friday, August 6th, 1221, at noon, Dominic Guzman died, as he had prayed to die, amidst his brethren of Bologna. Having no cell of his own, for "he had the whole world for cell," he died in the cell of one of the brethren. Having no clothes but those he wore, for "he had put on the Lord Jesus Christ," he died in the borrowed clothes of one of the brethren. It was the death of an apostle, fitly following the life of an apostle.

Few men of any age have been so qualified to be an apostle. His Spanish blood was of the best in Europe; but it was the best warrior blood. Many of the future dreams and ideals of the apostle may have been suggested to his mind by the grim frontier fortress of Calaroga, where he passed the first seven years of his life.

It is hard to find any saint, and especially any founder-saint, who was so essentially a cleric, that is, "a child of the Church." This was everything to him in the perilous days when he was adventuring into new ways of doing the Church's work of saving souls. At seven years old, when, as the theologians nobly say, "he had reached the age of reason," he left home with all its joys, for Gumiel d'Izan, when his uncle was Archpriest. He could hardly have known that he was beginning the long, hard apprenticeship of an apostle. Education in such a home of learning was essentially a learning of realities. Like many of his schoolfellows, the primer from which he learned his letters was the Book of Our Lady's Hours! Perhaps, as some of his schoolfellows, he had his first lesson from his Lady's Book, as it rested on her altar in the great church. The neighbouring Premonstratensian Abbey of Pena was too close to Gumiel d'Izan for us to neglect the Premonstratensian tradition that his youth was largely influenced by the Augustinian Rule. Perhaps it was there that, under the keeping of St. Augustine, he learned to love those songs of the Church which later on he was to sing to Europe as he travelled on his tireless apostolate.

It was well for Dominic Guzman that he passed from this Augustinian atmosphere to a university. Both these influences were characteristic of the Church of the twelfth and thirteenth centuries. The years he spent at Palencia amidst the students of the university completed his apprenticeship as a teacher and preacher of the Word of Truth.

From a worldly point of view the ecclesiastical career of Dominic Guzman was now achieved. His birth, his talents, his learning were a unique key which might be expected to open the door to the highest ecclesiastical dignities. Indeed, we may almost say that he took the first steps in his career when in his thirty-third year he was on a royal embassy to bring back the bride who was to have been his future queen.

A journey through Languedoc and a long night's victorious discussion with an Albigensian innkeeper suddenly awoke his apostolic heart. Not everyone who lives in "the whitening harvest-field of souls" can "lift up his eyes and see" that it is a harvest-field, and that it is white for reaping. It was not dismay but hope that thrilled the apostolic heart of St. Dominic when he realised two profound truths. The first was that the Ship of the Church was in danger of sinking; the second was that as the

danger had been brought about by men's, and especially
Churchmen's, sloth in using the covenanted boons of
God, the danger could be met only by a return to the
priceless heritage of God's truth and grace, that is, to
preaching and the sacraments. A kindred conviction was
reaching the kindred heart of the Umbrian Poverello. To
him it came by way of revelation, whereby he saw in a
mystic showing three churches almost in ruins. But the
mind of Dominic saw few revelations save those com-
pounded of his God-given faith and reason.

What manner of man Dominic the apostle seemed to
the men who knew him best may be judged by their
sworn witness after his death. The formal testimony
given before his canonization is a fragment of medieval
mysticism almost without rival. Throughout its legal
brevity and restraint may be felt the enthusiasm which
the children of Dominic Guzman still give to the Master
to whom they liken none but the giants and heroes of
the Church.

The witness of St. Dominic's fellow apostles is monoto-
nous in superlatives. Rudolf of Faenza: "Item. He said
that Dominic sought the salvation of all souls, both Chris-
tians and Saracens, and especially of the Cumans and
others. And he was the most zealous seeker after souls he
ever saw. And he often said he longed to go to the
Cumans and to the other nations." A more daring witness
was given by Fra Ventura: "He was such a lover of souls
that he stretched his charity and compassion not only to
the faithful, but even to the heretics and pagans and
even to the souls in hell. Greatly did he weep for them.
Great, too, was his fervour in preaching and in sending
others to preach."

His successor, Bd. Jordan of Saxony, himself one of the

most lovable saints and apostles of the thirteenth century, could write of his hero: "All men he welcomed within the wide bosom of his charity; and, since he loved all, he was beloved by all. To be glad with those that are glad, and to weep with those that weep, he took upon him as his right. He overflowed with mercy and outpoured himself wholly in the care of souls and in compassion for the sorrowing."

These witnesses have crystallized into phrases which give St. Dominic almost a place apart amongst the apostles: "He prayed God to place him as a stone in the mouth of hell, to keep sinners from falling therein. . . . No one ever looked upon him that did not love him." Though he lived and moved unarmed in the midst of the fierce Albigensians, none ever harmed him more than by cutting keepsakes from his habit, till it reached scarcely beyond his knee!

An apostle, so thought this authentic apostle, must be poor. He remembered the phrase of Dux Verbi: "as poor, yet enriching many." Rudolf of Faenza, the parish priest turned friar-preacher, who gave his church to the friars and watched over his hero as a mother watches her child, said with accustomed terseness: "I never saw him sleep in a bed of feather or on a mattress until he was dead. Then he lay on a mattress." A man who has no home, no cell, no change of clothing, no bed to lie on save the stone floor of his Lady's altar is after the image of Him Who had not whereon to lay His head.

Six times in a few years did Dominic walk across Europe in pursuit of souls. It is almost true to say of him that he sang his way across Europe. Yet it was never a song of his own composing he sang. All his songs were those of the Church—the Veni Creator Spiritus, the Ave

Maris Stella. St. Dominic was of those great souls who have no further desire than the Church's best. He composed no new song. He took care, like his Master, to leave no written rule or word of his own lest men should remember him!

But his children have remembered his desire to be forgotten and have never forgotten him. To them he is such a priceless heritage that they are jealous of sharing him with others who might give him only a lesser love. Seven hundred years of trial have done nothing to break the unity of Dominic's family; because in every crisis which threatened to break them apart they have remembered their Father and were one.

(From a Friar's Cell)

GILBERT KEITH CHESTERTON

THE DEATH of Gilbert Keith Chesterton—or "G.K.," as we called him—allows us to see his life as a complete and unique whole.

Looked at merely as a thing of art, the three score and two crowded years between birth in London and burial in Beaconsfield seem to make a full circle or indeed cycle of doings and happenings. Later on his autobiography will let us listen to the man who made the story telling the story or history he has made. But though every line of it will speak the master-craftsman of words, it will be a masterpiece in the humility of self-effacement. We have no hopes that it will deliberately help us to see his life's pilgrimage from London to Beaconsfield—from Canterbury to Rome—almost as an Arthurian epic.

For one thing we shall be grateful to the artist's portrait of himself. It will be a *vera effigies*. It will leave out nothing that would be a loss to truth. And though it cannot speak of how the artist's life ended in death, it will leave its readers convinced that death came to Gilbert Chesterton in a certain fulness of time and fulness of intelligence.

For us who are left there is deep consolation in the way he left us. We saw no slackening of his handiwork; nor any lessening of its power. He did not set slowly like our northern sun. He was as a ploughman turning his best and last furrow when the master said, "Call the workers;

and give them their wage." Then at a call he went home
to the peace which God in His courteousness calls a wage
and the worker in his humility calls a reward.

The dramatic unity of this life may one day give us a
theme as nobly framed and wrought as his own great
epic of the *White Horse*. But as only a reborn Shakespeare could dramatize the writer of *Hamlet,* we must
wait till a second Gilbert Chesterton comes before the
writer of the White Horse can be given dramatic justice.

◇ ◇ ◇ ◇

But Gilbert Chesterton's life was not merely a rounded
and complete whole; in more ways than one it was a
unique whole. The list of great sons whom England has
birthed since Shakespeare died has many who resembled
Gilbert Chesterton, but it has few who equal him. Perhaps this conviction of ours may become the conviction
of our readers if we change the manner of stating it. Instead of saying that in after-Shakespeare England many
have resembled without equalling Gilbert Chesterton,
we will say that Gilbert Chesterton has resembled many
even when this resemblance was not in a craft shared
equally by both.

His resemblance to Samuel Johnson was obvious in
things mental and literary, and was almost ludicrous in
the corporal sphere. Yet it was a greater than Johnson
who never wrote a *Letter to Lord Chesterfield;* but once
for ever followed up the good things he said about the
Church by humbly asking to share the good things of
the Church.

The writer of the *Outline of Sanity* is perhaps nearer
to Swift than to Johnson. Yet the layman sets an example
to the cleric in the complete banishment of the coarseness

and worse than coarseness which foul Swift's attempt at social reform.

An obvious and detected resemblance exists between Chesterton and Cobbett. Chesterton would have called it courteously the resemblance between himself a pupil and his master. Two things, however, make the master less than his pupil—too much self-assertion even in the assertion of fundamental truths, and too little self-assertion in not giving his *History of the Protestant Reformation* the needed imprimatur of his reception into the Catholic Church. That Cobbett never became a Catholic is an unwritten epilogue which almost discounts his *History*. But even Chesterton's strongest opponents felt that his reception into the Church was the one act needed to give unity to his thought and life.

These contrasts are not set down after the manner of Plutarch's, merely for the artistic aim of enforcing one colour by placing it side by side with an alternative. We have suggested that Gilbert Chesterton resembled many of his after-Shakespeare predecessors by possessing one or other of their qualities in a greater or equal degree. But he is contrasted with them in that he possessed within his mind and life the qualities of them all. Gilbert Chesterton was not just one thing, and that in its highest degree; he was many things, and that in a high degree. He was a born philosopher, a born poet, a born knight, and, I will make bold to say, a reborn saint.

◇ ◇ ◇ ◇

Few men of his age had more of the born philosopher in their thinking than the author of *The Everlasting Man* and *The Innocence of Father Brown*. It was perhaps well for him, and consequently well for us, that mere school-philosophy had no part in his schooling. His philosophy was that gradually deepening and unifying thing: "What Gilbert Chesterton thought about the Universe." It was not what Gilbert Chesterton thought that Bergson, or Darwin, or Hume, or Descartes, or Bacon, or Aquinas thought about the universe. But more and more it became what the Maker of the Universe thought about the Universe he had made. *Orthodoxy* and *The Everlasting Man* are sounder philosophical workmanship than Berkeley's *Dialogues* or Hume's *Essay on Miracles*. But they are as sound sterling English workmanship as *Lincoln Minster* or Shakespeare's *Hamlet*.

Chesterton's temporary connection with an English section of the Christian body, and indeed with a small subsection of that section, might have narrowed his outlook till it became parochial. Even the essentially philosophical mind of Newman did not avoid this danger. We may see the shadow of this narrowness in the *Apologia*, which, except for a few pages of profound thinking and many pages of flawless literature, might almost be labelled "Much ado about—Newman." But Newman's *Development of Doctrine* like Chesterton's *Orthodoxy* was the philosophy and the drama of truth asserting and uttering itself scientifically in battle with a thousand scientific heresies. And Newman's *Grammar of Assent* like Chesterton's *Everlasting Man* was an onslaught on the irrational intellectualism which despises the thought-ways of the average man in the street, or woman in the home.

Again, Chesterton's mind, so essentially philosophical, recognised that if a being is related to the Absolute, that relation is its absolute relation. It was not just the poet in him, it was first of all the philosopher in him that, when he walked the fields, saw in the daisy the eye of God, and,

when he sauntered abstractedly down the Strand, saw a
ladder stretching from heaven to Charing Cross.

◇ ◇ ◇ ◇

If any of my readers, after reading what Gilbert Chesterton wrote in verse, think that he is not one of our
English poets—perhaps the greatest and most English
of English ballad poets—I cannot hope that any words
of mine would be of avail. When his own words fail,
mine have no hope of success.

I can only say what I see, and see no less in Gilbert
Chesterton's prose than in his verse. There is hardly a
line of his writings that does not say to me with emphasis:
"This man is a philosopher." But there are few if any
lines that do not say with equal emphasis: "This philosopher is a poet."

The philosopher within him gives him the sense of line,
especially of the outline which is the accurate guardian
of totality and unity. But he has the colour sense as well
of words as of things. He recognises in words not merely
their meaning but their music. He sees the sun and moon
not merely as round but as shining.

Call it rhetoric if you will, but this wizard of words is
a fellow of the great captains when, almost against our
will, he calls up from our souls' deeps what emotions he
chooses to call.

◇ ◇ ◇ ◇

The philosopher and poet within Gilbert Chesterton
were but parts—and lesser parts—of a greater thing often
lacking in philosophers and poets. Gilbert Chesterton was
one of Nature's Knights whose philosophy could say

wise things for the scholar mind and whose poetry could offer sweet songs for the lips, but whose courage and courteousness could defend all weak, defenceless things except himself. Had some Kingsley attacked him as his fellow Londoner Newman was attacked, his reply would not have been an elaborate *Apologia pro vita sua*, but a great London laugh in which Kingsley, if only for humour's sake, would have joined.

Yet this man who was a child at self-defence was a dragon-slayer in defence of others. There is hardly a line he wrote, in prose or verse—for laughter or for anger or for tears—that is not Samson pulling down some embattled sanctuary of injustice or untruth. Many then who heard his challenging bugle calls turned a deaf ear to what they thought his despairing going back from the modern to the medieval. But they did not know that what Chesterton prized in past times was the eternal element of truth and justice which cannot pass. Moreover, it should have struck them that this

laudator temporis acti

was, at least in literature, so modern and so unlike past masters of literary style as to be a style in himself.

Like Shakespeare of the anti-Elizabethan, Essex group, he toiled with the pen in crusading against the enslavement of his contemporaries. Part of his unique character is that the crusading field had widened since the days when a Cecil-led aristocracy held a Sovereign and a people in bondage. Chesterton could not be contemporary of Marx, The Great War, the Russian Experiment, without seeing the social question to be, what Leo XIII stated it to be, "the Pressing Question of the hour." [1] He was

---

[1] Pope Leo XIII, *Rerum Novarum.*

one of the few who accepted the Pope's invitation "to strive to secure the good of the people, and to bring to the struggle the full energy of his mind."

It is this combination in one life of Philospher, Poet and Social Knight that made Gilbert Chesterton's life and life's work in many ways unique. In his *Return of Don Quixote* and in his *Essay on Dickens* he has suggested a view of his life's work which is true though not complete. Dickens had doubtless in mind Don Quixote and Sancho Panza when he wrote his immortal *Pickwick Papers*. At any rate Mr. Pickwick and Sam Weller are a Cockney Don Quixote and Sancho Panza.

Yet there was little of Don Quixote in Cervantes; still less of Mr. Pickwick in Dickens. But we can hardly express the bulk and quality of Gilbert Chesterton's work without saying that he was Cervantes, and Dickens, and Don Quixote, and Sancho Panza, and Mr. Pickwick, and Sam Weller—and Johnson, and Swift, and Cobbett—in one!

Moreover, the man in him was greater than the thinking man, or the singing man, or the crusading man. He himself was so much better than anything he wrote or did that his words and deeds were but symbols of the inner source of all he said or did. In this he differs from a crowd of writers, and statesmen, whose achievements in word or deed are only admirable by us, whilst we shut out from our thoughts the memory of the men they were.

It was this visible oneness of the worker and his work that made this London-born philosopher, poet, knight, England's *de facto* if not *de jure* ambassador to the world. His death was felt as a blow and fitly mourned not merely at Beaconsfield where he died, and at Westminster near to where he was born, but wherever letters and culture and courtesy were found.

◊ ◊ ◊ ◊

With this thought we have come to the most delicate and therefore deliberate thing we have to say about the man Gilbert Chesterton. Whilst not using the word sanctity as synonymous with that verifiable heroic virtue which receives official authentication, we cannot complete what we feel should be said about him without using the word sanctity or holiness. Holiness, at least in the English form, denotes a certain *wholeness* which the rounded and complete life of Chesterton suggests to our thought. A saint or holy man is in part a philosopher who, in even the least of beings related to God, sees the One Absolute, and in that One sees all. A saint is in part a poet who sees and feels such beauty of line and colour in God's handiworks that he worships God in them with the rhythm and imagery, the line and colour, of his verse. A saint is in part a knight so enamoured of the First Good that every evil thing challenges him to combat under his Sovereign's eye. Now for Gilbert Chesterton this Sovereign under whose eye and for whose glory he fought was the First Truth, the Most Fair, the Highest Good—Lord of lords and King of kings.

This subtle quality of *wholeness* in his mind's aim and soul's desire can be fitly expressed only by such a phrase as St. Paul wrote "to the saints" at Philippi: "Our citizenship (πολίτευμα) is in heaven." Gilbert Chesterton, like the little world-wandering Jew of Tarsus, dwelt primarily in Heaven, even as a lad in Kensington, or amidst fellowjournalists in Fleet Street, or as chairman of a Distributist meeting, or in a debate with an agnostic, or at his own hearth at Beaconsfield.

This constant abiding with what was highest in human thought and desire gave him that indescribable but unmistakable character of humility. Gilbert Chesterton, whom the present writer reckons one of the greatest sons born to England for three hundred years, was a humble man. Indeed only a man of tried humility could have written:

> The firm feet of humility
> That grip the ground like trees.

He had the first effect or endowment of humility expressed by his Master: "*Learn* of Me for I am . . . humble of heart." He could learn. He could learn as quickly as a child because by an achievement of genius and sanctity he had a child's simplicity of thought. From the countless expressions of this achieved simplicity I pick one at random.

> "Don't you think," asked Muriel, "that modern things are too complicated to be dealt with in such a simple way."
> "I think," replied Hearne, "that modern things are too complicated to be dealt with except in a simple way."
> (*The Return of Don Quixote*)

So essentially was he a learner that everyone, even his opponents (for enemy he had none), had something to teach him. He was thus not only the *servus servorum*, making all he met his masters whom in love he served, but making them all his teaching-masters from whom in gratitude he learned.

Another high activity of this humble soul was its gentle, winsome self-apology. He never shirked unambiguous assertion of the truth; yet the many volumes he has written will have to be screened fine to yield one phrase of self-assertion. We can imagine that on coming to full consciousness of the earth and sun he apologized to the earth for taking up so much room, and asked pardon of the sun for casting so wide and deep a shadow. He even seemed to make amends for the burial trouble he gave us by making his burial day one of sunshine in a summer of clouds and rain.

So knit were his mind and soul with God that his very laughter—so frequent and so infectious—had a quality almost liturgical. It seemed in its own human way a ritual worship of the Truth. He could have called himself what the writer of Utopia called himself: "God's giglot." But he had ". . . Wisdom for motley; truth for loving jest."

Another master-activity of this humble soul was his unruffled patience. One incident may suffice. At the Eucharistic Congress in Dublin he sat beside a priest whilst a Bishop gave an hour's address in Gaelic. At the end of the hour, during which he had been almost motionless, he heaved a smile and said, with a characteristic chuckle: "The finer points of that discourse escaped me." That smile and whimsicality were the fine, patient craftsmanship of humility.

A quality at once felt but not at once analyzable in the thought of St. Thomas Aquinas is to be found in the words of Gilbert Chesterton. With both men thought becomes consecration: their intellectual activities have a dominantly moral character. The finest quality about their mental work is not its truth, but its moral worth, its goodness—indeed its holiness. Their common mental sanity is an intellectual flowering of their deeper sanctity of soul. Compared with St. Thomas, Gilbert Chesterton is as

David, dancing before the Ark, compared to one of the steady-moving levites on whose shoulders the Ark was borne. But levite by his up-bearing shoulders, and king by his dancing feet, equally worshipped God.

This was the reason why it was hard to speak with Gilbert Chesterton and not to think—and think of God. Even the atheist who spoke with him, and who would have despised the God of Abraham, the God of Isaac, the God of Jacob, felt he would like to know about the God of Gilbert Chesterton—this God whom the very laughter of Gilbert Chesterton seemed to prove was such a lovably human, though transcendant, a being that doubt had a crucifixion denied to faith.

Some few days after we had buried him fitly amidst "sunshine and English meadow-flowers" I heard the word I longed, and God meant me, to hear. Someone who knew him well came to speak to me of spiritual difficulties. I had felt that the death of Gilbert Chesterton would be accompanied by some quiet sign of God's "Well done" to His tireless apostle. The name that was in both our minds at last was spoken, and I heard what I had a dim premonition I should hear: "You know, Father, I often wanted to make my Confession to him. He would have understood."[2]

If, then, the world everywhere is speaking of his genius and we are speaking confidently of his humility, we are confidently giving him a unique place in the history of his birth-town or, indeed, his birth-land. Since the death of

[2] I think I once delighted him by telling him a kindred incident about an old Mr. Morris whom, after his most holy life and death, I buried at Leicester. He was one of Nature's most finished gentlemen, who had changed wealth for poverty with a dignity befitting the first of the beatitudes. Before he finally left his native Ireland an old charwoman said of him: "If ever there was a saint, 'tis the master. Sure he could bless your beads!"

his fellow Londoner Thomas More the Catholics of England, and therefore England, has been given no great man-child whose life bore the quartering of philosophy, poetry, chivalry and holiness. But St. Thomas More came to life again when Chesterton was born. Thus the Lord giveth, and the Lord taketh away, then the Lord giveth again to reassure us, lest in mourning our heroes and saints who are dead we forget that God is not dead; nor has He lost His power "from the stones to raise up children to Abraham."

(*Blackfriars,* Vol. XVII)

Verse

ROSA PATIENTIAE

The rose's hue and scent
　　Are meant,
By Him Who made the rose, to adorn
　　A thorn.

And thus, when sorrow irks,
　　Who shirks
Forgets to count the gain
　　Of pain—
Nor, joy-benighted, knows
　　The rose.

(Blackfriars, Vol. XIII)

FOLLOW ME

Out of Life's meadows bright with Spring,
　　Out of the woods whose cloister long
　　The throstle fills with love-born song,
Out of thy youth's illusioning
　　Follow Me.

Down through Life's thickets where the briar
　　Thy childhood's gossamer may rend,
　　Down through a darkness where the end
Is reached through floods of sea and fire
　　Follow Me.

Up to Golgotha,—a tree
　　Where hangs thy Love in piteous rue,
　　Then up! where Jesu's wounds embrue
Thy soul with endless ecstacy
　　Follow Me.

(Blackfriars, Vol. IX)

CANTICUM MAGORUM

The crib and stable
Are not man's fable;

But are in sooth
God's naked Truth.

The narrow cave
Is what God gave
Our pride to save.

The mirk within
Is mortal sin.

The winter frost
Is God's love lost.

The hay and straw
Are things of awe,
Befall'n by law.

Ev'n ox and ass
Have come to pass.

The want and cold
Are pain foretold.

The Nursling's cries
End prophecies.

The star without
Has come about
To light our doubt.

The working man
Kneels there, to plan.

And, man of faith
All joyous saith:

'That Son Who stirs
Is God's and—hers!'

The Maid who sings
Soft carollings

Lulls by her words
The LORD OF LORDS.

From out the skies
Loud anthems rise.

Heav'n's royal choir
A song conspire
All shot with fire,

To speed their King
Gone conquering.

And we who now
Before Thee bow

Are wholly sin
Without, within.

Yet—crib and stable
Being no fond fable,

Although our guilt
This Child's joy spilt,

Our hearts beat wild
To know this Child

Is GOD THE SON
AND SIN—UNDONE!

ERO MORS TUA O MORS.
(*Blackfriars*, **Vol. VI**)

SAINT THOMAS

Angel in mind and heart! thy fervent soul
  Was filled with love and high poetic song:
  Peopling thy fancy, dwelt a mighty throng
Of harmonies divine. Thou could'st control
Such floods of heavenly minstrelsy as roll
  Through minds angelic. Swiftest glance among
  The things of God inspired thee. High and long
Thou chanted'st Panges—anthems sweet that stole
Men's hearts for God. Say then, bard of Christ hid,
  How thou could'st limn God, the All-Fair, how press
  Jesu's piercéd side, th'ensanguined wounds caress
Of Christ, tearless and songless; how forbid
  Thy heart its throbs—it's rue, lest Truth divine
  Should stain its limpid rills with aught of thine?
                  (*Blackfriars*, Vol. V)

NON NISI TE, DOMINE [1]

I

God of all kindness! from the abyss of nought
  To this fair world of land and sea
  With billow crowned and waving tree,
By Thee in love eternal was I brought,—
  Was brought by Thee;—none else but Thee.

II

And now within this slowly dying heart
  My childhood's dreams steal back to me,
  As when I sought to pierce and see,
Behind the veils of sight, if but in part,
  One glimpse of Thee;—none else but Thee.

III

These parchments with their finely fretted lines
  My failing eyes no more may see,

[1] Reply of St. Thomas Aquinas to Our Blessed Lord.

How tranquill was the ecstacy
They brought, like coolest draught to one who pines
  Athirst for Thee;—none else but Thee.

IV

Then when the golden morn of youth had passed
  To manhood's day; and bold and free
  I read the world's philosophy,
Its first clear-sounding message as its last
  But spoke of Thee;—none else but Thee.

V

And then how yearned my soul the glad good tidings
  Unto the world's deep misery
  To forth-tell, that humanity
Might spurn at last its low and selfish guidings
  And yield to Thee:—none else but Thee.

VI

I wrote for men; and intercourse with men
  With aims so low and destiny
  Of angels, made the mystery
Of life darker and darker still;—and then
  I groped for Thee:—none else but Thee.

VII

Thee had I clasped and held with childhood's love,
  And handled all too fearlessly
  With youth's impetuosity
Till the world's noon-day seemed from heaven above
  To banish Thee;—none else but Thee.

VIII

Yet wrote on I in never waning trust
  With faith that brought the tears from me
  With hope that drained the life from me;
And taught man he is but a grain of dust
  Yet made for Thee;—none else but Thee.

IX

How ill I taught, the blessed vision now
  Vouchsafed brings home so piercingly!
  All is but chaff I wrote; and, see,
In ignorance and pride most headstrong how
  I mis-spoke Thee;—none else but Thee.

X

What hear I, Lord? Canst Thou so soon forget
  My wilful past and summon me
  To ask reward! Then shall it be,
God of my youth and when my sun is set!
  None else but Thee;—none else but Thee.

                  (*Blackfriars,* Vol. IX)

≫≫≫≫≫

Apologetics and Theology

≫≫≫≫≫

CONFESSION TO A PRIEST

〜〜〜〜〜

I AM GOING to speak to my reader as man to man.

When one man speaks to his fellow man the first thing he owes to his hearer is Truth. Lying, which kills truth, kills fellowship.

When one man listens to his fellow man the first thing he owes to him is Trust. Everyone should be trusted as telling the truth until he is found to lie. Especially may he be trusted as telling the truth if a lie did him no good.

Now if I ask my reader to trust me in telling the truth about Confession it is because a lie would do me no good. Indeed it would be to my hurt, for I should have to go to Confession and confess: "In writing about Confession I told deliberate lies."

◊ ◊ ◊ ◊

You may be one of those who think that Confession is only a Roman Catholic practice. You may even be one of those who believe that Confession is a device of the Roman Catholic priests for getting money out of an ignorant laity.

Now the truth is that Confession is not just a Roman Catholic practice. It is a Christian practice. You will find it in all the old Christian bodies of the East. All the Christian Churches of the world believed that Confession was instituted by Jesus Christ. This belief was not challenged until Luther and the so-called "Reformers" denied it.

Therefore anyone calling himself a Christian must give a reason why he pits himself against the whole group of Christian bodies by rejecting Confession.

◊ ◊ ◊ ◊

You may possibly be of opinion that only the laity, and not the priests, go to Confession.

No! even the priests go to Confession. Indeed, even the Pope goes to Confession. Though we Catholics hold that Popes are officially infallible, they are not personally impeccable. They can commit sin like the rest of us. Moreover, other things being equal, their sins are worse than ours. But if they can personally commit sin they cannot forgive their own sin. Indeed Popes are, perhaps, the only persons who proclaim their sinfulness from the house-top.

◊ ◊ ◊ ◊

You will probably find the word SIN seldom used in the papers and books that you read. Yet, though it is one of the smallest words in the English language, it is one of the most necessary. For example, you are very likely interested in the social difficulty. Perhaps you have never realised that in the English language, as in every language, only the word SIN sums up the difficulty. If you wished to sum up in one word the present social evil, there would be only one word to use—sin.

Why? Because the word SIN means "a bad act of man's free will." So that if you think of it, what is wrong in the world is not "heredity or environment," as is so often said, but bad human wills. No wonder that when He, who was called the Prince of Peace, was born in a stable with the cattle, angels in the heavens sang: "Peace on earth to men of good will." Hence "wars on earth come from men of bad will."

Perhaps you have been struck by the objection often found on the lips of sincere Protestants. You may say: "I am a believer in Jesus Christ and in the Bible. Yet search as I can, I have never found that Jesus told us we must confess our sins to a priest."

Let me say at once that I have deep sympathy with those who sincerely hold this opinion. Ever since the new religions came from Luther and his fellows, men have gone on this principle, "Religion is something we get out of a book"—just as out of a navigation book we find out how to navigate, and out of a cookery book we learn how to cook.

But religion is not something we get out of a book. On the contrary, "Religion is something we put into a book." I need not say that religion being a great thing cannot be wholly put into any book. A follower of Jesus said that if he tried to write all that Jesus did the whole world itself would not be able to contain the books that should be written.

Now no book was ever written so fully and so clearly that nowhere did it need to be made clearer for the average reader.

Therefore when Luther and his fellows told men to get their religion out of a book without heeding the Church, the writer of the Book, he was responsible for what you may now be thinking about Confession.

I will ask you to listen whilst I tell you the meaning of the Book on this matter of Confession. You will listen all the readier when you realise that I am not giving you my opinion about the Book. I guarantee to give you only the opinion of (the Church) the writer of the Book.

(1) Jesus Christ once said quite plainly: "Except you eat the flesh of the Son of man and drink His blood, you shall not have life in you."

This is a clear command to receive Communion, whatever that Communion may mean.

Moreover, whoever disobey this command "shall not have life in their soul." In other words, they will commit grievous sin.

(2) You will say: "I agree. But I do not find that Jesus has given us a command to confess our sins."

Now I am glad you say this, because I may be able to give you, not an answer, but THE answer. "Jesus Christ, in His merciful plan of making a Church for average folk, did not give us this command."

The Church teaches us that we are not bound to tell all our sins in Confession. We are bound to tell in Confession only our grievous sins. Confession is not so much a duty as a privilege.

Hence if our soul is not dead with grievous sin, we are not bound to go to Confession.

Take this truth and add to it this other truth: With God's ordinary help we can live without committing grievous sin. When you have added these two truths together you will see that Jesus did not wish to command us to go to Confession, as He commanded us to go to Communion.

(3) But He clearly allowed us to go to Confession. Moreover He rewarded our humility in confessing our sins. Catholics know that Jesus made Confession into a Sacrament for giving the soul of man supernatural help to reach the supernatural end of its natural life. We say again: Confession is not a duty except for grievous sin. But Confession, by giving grace, is a privilege.

If you are a Christian read again and read on your knees the scene recorded by the disciple whom Jesus loved: ". . . breathed on them, and saith to them: Receive ye the Holy Ghost; whose sins ye forgive they are forgiven unto them: whose sins ye retain, they are retained." [1]

Words could not be plainer. If we do not accept their plain meaning, God will ask us to show reason for not accepting. It will be difficult for us to say we believe in Jesus, and also say that we do not accept the plain words of Jesus.

(4) To sum up. As with God's ordinary help we need not commit grievous sin; we need not go to Confession. Therefore Jesus did not command us to go to Confession.

But when Jesus gave to His Church the power of forgiving sins, and of giving grace, He offered us a help which millions of souls are glad to seek and to have.

◇ ◇ ◇ ◇

There used to be some folk who thought and said that Catholics went to Confession in order to get leave to commit sin.

I hope you are not one of these folk. If you are one of those who think we Catholics go to Confession in order to get leave to commit sin I can only say, "We don't."

If you do not believe me ask any ordinary Catholic man you know. But be careful whom you ask. I have known unpleasant consequences!

◇ ◇ ◇ ◇

Again I hope you are not one of those who think that money payment must be made for Confession.

[1] John 20:22.

Let me tell you a true incident. When my brother Lawrence was studying medicine at Durham University, a Protestant fellow student, no doubt wishing to rag him in front of a group of students, said, "McNabb, how much do you pay for Confession?"

He was answered sooner than he expected by my brother saying with his usual emphatic quiet: "Four-pence halfpenny—three pence for the priest and three halfpence for his wife!"

I think I can leave you to see why he was not asked questions like that for some time.

Personally I have been going to Confession for some sixty-seven years. I have never paid, and I never intended to pay a farthing. During all that time I have sought and received the most valuable advice for nothing. Had I sought and received as much (though less valuable) advice from a lawyer, I think I should now be an insolvent bankrupt.

◇ ◇ ◇ ◇

You may be too young to remember the slogans which were on everybody's lips during and after the Great War. Some of these slogans had such a fate that they don't bear remembering. I believe President Woodrow Wilson was responsible for perhaps the most famous slogan, which seemed then to be the spirit of the Versailles peace-makers. Please don't laugh when I tell you that this slogan from Versailles was, "We must make the world safe for Democracy."

No doubt you have your own opinion about the fate or even the fact of this Versailles effort to give Democracy a chance. With that opinion of yours I will not interfere, because all during my years of priesthood I have never given a party-political opinion; and indeed never had a political opinion to give. My priestly job has been the hard task of keeping to the ethical principles which no political opinions can flout.

But it is many years since I saw that Democracy stands or falls with the practice of Confession.

Let me put it this way to you. I presume that Democracy means the government of free men by themselves; the so-called ruling class in a Democracy are merely the delegates of the people. As delegates these rulers or officials cannot go beyond the terms of their commission.

The sovereignty of free men over their freely-chosen delegates is based on the great political principle that men are born free, and that only for some crime against their fellow man can that freedom be taken away.

This is what is rightly called "Political Freedom." It is called a right. But as no one or no group has a right to do wrong this political freedom of a Democracy must work inside what is morally right and not morally wrong.

I think you are beginning to see that the political freedom of men must rest on the personal freedom or free will of man, whereby man is not just a physical, but also a moral, being. The next time you go to the Zoological Gardens you can ask any of the inhabitants—the monkeys or the elephants or the crocodiles—whether they are in favour of a Democracy. Even if they could understand English they could not understand the question you put in English. Why? Because they have no free will. "Free" means as little to them as "red, white, and blue" mean to a man born blind.

Now begin to think all that would be meant if you

went and told your sins to these inhabitants of the Zoo, e.g.: "I was very angry. I beat my wife. I was unfaithful to my wife. I stole things from the canteen," etc., etc.

I need not say that none of the inhabitants of the Zoo would understand you. Still less would they imitate you by confessing their sins. Monkeys have been trained (by the intelligence of men) to do a number of things which seem to show intelligence. But, trained or not trained, no monkey has ever been known to accuse itself of having stolen the nuts of the family or having been rude to its aged grandparents. Why? Because no monkey has free will.

But if ever you knelt down accusing yourself of having done wrong you would mean that you were responsible for doing wrong because you could have done right. In other words your self-accusation would mean the conviction that you had the moral power to do right and wrong. In other words, you as good as said, "I am a free man." You therefore made a humble and noble declaration of liberty, more fundamental than that which is so nobly incorporated in the American Constitution, and in the colossal statue in the river approach to New York.

I feel sure that when you think of Democracy you also think of free men electing by means of a ballot box. But when you have gone to Confession as often as I have gone, and when you have loved freedom as much as I have loved it, you will say what I have now said these many years: "For safeguarding Liberty and Democracy the ballot box is not so effective as the confessional box."

Let me tighten up this principle by telling an incident of my own experience.

Some years ago I accepted a challenge from a Glasgow

Communist to debate the subject: Christianity Is No Use to the Working Classes.

It was a record meeting. About 2,000 could not find a seat in the largest hall in Glasgow. My adversary, who, I was told, had once been a Protestant lecturer, made his opening speech a continued attack on the Catholic practice of Confession. To this day I cannot find the reason for this attack; except perhaps that being hurried at the last moment he fell back on an old Protestant lecture. For some time whilst he was making his opening speech I was so bewildered by what cricketers would call his wide bowling that I could not see how I could deal with it, or could deal with an audience who saw any argument in it.

Almost during his last few sentences did I see some chance not only of defending myself against an aimless attack but even of turning this attack on me into an attack on him.

The great coal strike had only ceased a few days before our meeting. The Communists of the Clyde district, who were the most powerful Communist group in these islands, saw the strike and their hopes ended by a very determined government action. Almost to a man they were still sore at what they called a ruthless defeat.

So when I stood up to reply to my adversary I stood smiling as I said: "My adversary has said a great deal about going to Confession. I presume he means that it would be of no service to the working-man if men had to go to Confession when they had done very wrong.

"Now you are all feeling sore about the unjust way the Cabinet have succeeded in ending this working-man's strike. But don't you think that it might have been

good for the working-men if these Cabinet Ministers had
had to go to Confession?

"Once an English king, Henry II, had to go to Confession after slaying one of his subjects, Thomas à Becket.
After he confessed his sin, his penance meant that he
was scourged by one of the Canterbury monks."

I finished by suggesting that a new era of hope for the
working classes would dawn in these islands when German-made Protestantism was ousted, and politicians of
even Cabinet rank might find that the Christian institution of Confession was so effective an instrument of social
justice that they ran the risk of a public scourging.

I think my adversary as well as my audience felt the
scourge-like force of the reply. At any rate neither the
audience nor I heard any more about Confession. For
this reason I say, and perhaps one day you will say, that
Democracy, now so endangered, will be saved by the confessional box rather than the ballot box.

◊ ◊ ◊ ◊

Perhaps it was this historic meeting in the vast Glasgow
hall that took me from Confession to Democracy; and
then beyond. How often when I spoke at street corners
and in public parks have I heard the average Protestant
objector: "Why need you confess to man? I confess my
sins to God alone; because God alone can forgive my
sins."

I own that for some years after first hearing this objection it seemed to have some impressiveness. Of course believing, with my fellow-Catholics, that Jesus was God and
that He had given His priests the power to forgive sin
(but not their own sins!) I knew that the objection was
wrong. Yet I suffered the mental strangle hold of not see-

ing how it was wrong. Gradually some years of thinking brought into my mind a light which, I pray God, may be brought into your mind.

(1) This light began to dawn in my mind when I dimly realised what was meant by the Christian doctrine of the Brotherhood of Man.

I say advisedly "The Christian doctrine" of the Brotherhood of Man for two reasons: first, it was Jesus Christ who first taught His followers to go into all nations with the good tidings of redemption. In God's dealings with mankind as such there were no privileged classes or favoured nations.

This Brotherhood of Man is often and rightly said to be grounded on the Brotherhood of God. But it is doubly grounded on the Brotherhood of God.

We who hold that Jesus Christ is true God, and further hold that He became our brother in the flesh, must hold, with joy, that God is our brother.

Perhaps the most striking sign that God looks on all men as His brothers, is found in the last address which Jesus gave to the world before He was crucified. Fitly this last address was on the Last Judgment which the Maker of mankind will pass on the lifeworks of men.

When judging that the good shall come into His kingdom He grounds His judgment on the fact that the good gave Him food and drink and clothing and shelter and care and mercy. When the good are bewildered by this list of good deeds which they are unconscious of having done, He says: "Amen I say to you, as long as you did it to one of these MY LEAST BRETHREN you did it to ME." [1]

No wonder that within a few years after the death of the Speaker of these words the Asiatic, Paul of Tarsus,

[1] Matt. 25:40.

writes to the cultured Greeks, whose culture rested on slavery: "In one Spirit were we all baptized into one body, whether Jews or Gentiles, whether bondsmen or freemen."[2]

(2) Our second reason for looking on the Christian origin of mankind as a Brotherhood of Man is grounded on the Sacrifice of the New Testament which fulfills and therefore annuls the sacrifices both of Jew and Gentile.

To realise this sign of the Brotherhood of Man, begin by realising that a Brotherhood must be, in some sense, a group of equals.

Yet the startling fact about men is their inequalities of nature and opportunity. These inequalities are so great in themselves that they produce the most startling inequalities in the social life of man.

Now go through the sumptuous halls of a bank, or the hardly less sumptuous halls of a modern university, or the halls and committee rooms of a modern parliament, or the doubly-guarded room of a modern dictator. Having gone through these undeniable signs of the inequalities of man, pass into a Catholic church during the hour of the Sunday morning sacrifice: all classes, as the world ranks classes, are there before the one altar: and are there not indeed as identical but as equal.

The inequalities of men are still there. Moreover viewed in themselves and in their worldly effects these inequalities are very great. But before that altar on which God-made-man is mystically slain these inequalities are viewed, not in themselves but in the presence of the Infinite. Think of what you see. Soon your mind will see it is only in the presence of the infinitely Great that the inequalities of men are seen to be infinitely small.

[2] I Cor. 12:1,3.

Before the altar on which God proves His love of all men, His brothers, all men are equal, because equally His brothers.

(3) You may need some time to realise this fact, e.g., that only in the Catholic Sunday sacrifice is there the effective Brotherhood of Man. Elsewhere are to be found the name and claim: but the claim is groundless and the name has been borrowed from those writings which have often been looked on as not worth writing or reading.

When you have sufficiently realised that mankind is (or should be!) a Brotherhood of Man, don't shirk certain conclusions because you shirk the duty they lay upon you.

You cannot admit on the one hand that you are one of a great world-wide Brotherhood and, on the other hand, deny that your acts and even your thoughts made you responsible to this Brotherhood. If

> . . . thou canst not pluck a flower
> Without troubling a star

your acts and even your thoughts, which are the seeds of your acts, are a help or hurt to the Brotherhood. No need to labour this truth with men whom their beloved country has called to its defence. Few societies are so much a body as a people's army. But every good soldier in that army knows that even the acts of his time of leave have some effect and may even have a great effect on the final issue of the war which called him to the army from his home.

Thus, in the almost overwhelming attack of the German army in 1914, the success of 1940 was just missed because in the rapidly advancing right flank of the Germans Foch found and widened a gap. But there are historians of the war who say that this gap, or failure to keep time in the hurried advance, was due to the slackness of a regiment whose officers had drunk more wine than their wearied brains could stand. Their personal delay over their cups meant four years of slaughter and the defeat of their country.

(4) Here I will ask you to think over one of the most socially fundamental principles Jesus Christ ever proclaimed. If Jesus Christ was not something greater than a revolutionary, indeed, so great that we have no name for it, we might think that no more revolutionary principle had ever been proclaimed. Let me set it down with all the emphasis of capital letters.

> IF THOU OFFER THY GIFT AT THE ALTAR, AND THERE
> THOU REMEMBER
> THAT THY BROTHER HATH ANYTHING AGAINST THEE;
> LEAVE THERE THY OFFERING BEFORE THE ALTAR,
> AND GO FIRST TO BE RECONCILED TO THY BROTHER:
> AND THEN COMING THOU SHALT OFFER THY GIFT.[1]

Notice how the Crucified speaks only of Brother! Mankind is a Brotherhood in Him; their Brother.

Notice again, the little word FIRST. God who has made us and our neighbour is not served unless we first serve our neighbour. In other words the God we serve is One who says by His prophet: "My soul hateth your new moons and your solemnities. I am weary of bearing them. Take away the evil of your devices from my eyes. Cease to do perversely. Learn to do well. Relieve the oppressed. Judge for the fatherless. Defend the widow." [2]

This God, whom alone we could, and do, serve is a God of Justice. Hence if every act of ours has an effect on the Brotherhood every grievous act has some grievous effect

[1] Matt. 5:23–24.
[2] Isaias 1:14–17.

on the Brotherhood. And God's forgiveness awaits the
Brotherhood's forgiveness.

Let me make this clearer by an example. If I stole £50
from you I should have committed a grievous sin—against
God because against you. If I say to God, "I have sinned
against Thee, forgive me," God will say, "You have sinned
against your neighbour. I cannot, in justice, forgive you
until you have paid back what you stole; or until your
neighbour forgives you." If my sin against you were forgiven merely by saying privately to God, "I am sorry," He
would be a God of injustice and therefore not God.

Now if our grievous acts are a grievous hurt to the
Brotherhood of Man we must seek and receive the forgiveness of the Brotherhood. This forgiveness of the
Brotherhood we cannot receive from the millions of men
and women in the world. But even as we deal with social
bodies when we deal with their official representative so
too we can receive from the official representatives of the
Brotherhood the official necessary forgiveness of the
Brotherhood.

In establishing an official priesthood from the midst of
the Brotherhood, Jesus appointed official representatives
not only of Himself but also of the Brotherhood.

In other words, were our soul alone with God and without God-made neighbours our sins need be confessed to
God alone. But now that God has made our neighbours,
whom we injure by our evil acts, the evil acts or sins must
be confessed not only to God but to our neighbour.

Profound social teaching is in the arrangement which
Jesus made for Confession and Communion. The equal
Brotherhood of Man is as the Sacrifice of God-made-man.
But the full fellowship of that Brotherhood is not granted
to those whose acts have grievously hurt the Brotherhood

until the forgiveness of the Brotherhood has been granted by its God-appointed representative in Confession.

◇ ◇ ◇ ◇

One last word to those who may hesitate to entrust the secret of their grievous faults to a fellow man; and indeed to a fellow sinner. When Jesus organised a priesthood to hear and absolve from sin, He forbade the one who hears the sin ever to make known what he knows only through his priesthood. When as a child of seven I made my first Confession to Fr. Daniel McCashin at his knees and in his sitting room, St. Malachy's College, Belfast, I knew that what I had told him was a divine secret entrusted to him. No power on earth could compel him to say what I had said. Rather than reveal the sins confessed by a little lad of seven years he would have to suffer death. That I knew; and that helped me to tell him what, perhaps, I had never told before.

Doctors might discuss the question, "Should a doctor tell?" Doctors might even agree that rather than be committed for contempt of court by a civil court they could tell.

But priests never discuss "Should a priest tell, if threatened with contempt of court by a civil judge?" Higher than a civil judge sitting in an earthly court there is an Eternal Judge and Saviour who had told His (good) shepherds that for love of Him, who has commissioned them by His power and encouraged them by His death, they must be ready to lay down their life for His flock.

◇ ◇ ◇ ◇

And now, dear reader, if you cannot as yet join with millions of your fellow men in telling your sins and your sorrow for sin to the representative of mankind, perhaps you may feel able to join them in the simple words expressing the sorrow they feel for their sin:

O my God. I am very sorry for having offended You, because You are so good; and I will not sin again.

THE SCRUPLE OF DOUBT

IT IS not the aim of this conference to deal with that extreme form of doubting which denies the existence or the rationality of all certitude except the certitude that everything is involved in doubt. It is consoling to reassure ourselves, on the word of psychologists, that such extreme scepticism could never be a lasting intellectual state. Whether or not such thorough-going sceptics are to be found outside our philosophical textbooks, they would assuredly be found to be far beyond the reach of any logical process either of persuasion or refutation. Their inconsequence, as it saves them from the ill effects of any application of their principle to daily life, would also protect them from anything that could be urged in favour of a reconsideration or rejection of their principle.

Nor shall we come to closer quarters with those other minds who embrace a partial scepticism in this or that department of religious thought. There are not a few who link their acceptance of revealed religion and even of Christianity with a denial of one or other point of dogma. Whilst accepting the infallibility of the Bible they scruple to admit the infallibility of the Church. They admit the change of water into wine at Cana of Galilee, but deny transubstantiation. They see no difficulty in admitting that Baptism cleanses from original sin, but cannot see that any sacrament could remit mortal sin. They admit the Sacrament of Penance, which forgives the guilt of sin, and reject indulgences, which merely profess to deal, not with guilt, but with punishment. They admit the doctrine of Christ's divinity, and reject the real presence. To such as these we shall make no formal appeal; though some of the principles which will come up for explanation will doubtless meet their psychological state.

The thoughts which will be raised in this conference will be mainly meant for that large number of sincere thinkers who scruple to accept the supernatural. These men conceive it highly immoral to consent to the truths that lie at the root or on the summit of Christian Revelation. They refuse to stir outside the region of facts into what they would term a penumbra of theory. To assent to the immortality of the soul, or to the existence of a personal God, or to the incarnation of the second person of the Blessed Trinity, or to the real presence, would seem to them a reckless submergence of the powers which nature has given them for the pursuit of truth. It is enough for them to find their minds brought into touch with what are generally called facts. They find their happiness sufficiently provided for in the positive sciences which, long looked upon as worked out, have yielded such treasure during the past century. In their more emotional moods they are prompted to ask why men should fret themselves to detect and analyze the dim shadows of their fancy, when the full and living realities of the world in all their uncounted richness are all around. "Why," they exclaim, "should a man distress himself with such wraith-lore as immortality and incarnation and infallibility, when he may walk abroad and rejoice in the great mathematical, physical, and biological sciences which have proved such inexhaustible mines of knowledge?"

Nay, more, they will boldly hold, and no less boldly teach, that to go beyond our data, to put more into our conclusions than we find in our premises, to begin with physical phenomena and end with metaphysical entities, to lay a foundation of material beings and to build up an edifice or hierarchy of spiritual substances, to start from a standpoint of likelihood or probability and to arrive at the absolute certitude of faith, is a process equally opposed to the normal action of the understanding and the moral action of the will. Nor, as they will add, ought a man to be tempted to the folly of belief by the acknowledged restfulness of believing. Only when peace, not duty, has become the aim of life, may a man supplement the facts which he knows by the theories he would believe. Those who will not be ensnared into chanting the Credo by any promise of "Peace to men," are asked to share the blessed lot of such as cannot sin against the truth, by calling the darkness of human knowledge the broad day of divine certainty. And though their devotion to truth cuts them off from a very world of thought, to them it is a world of dreams which any man can enter if he choose, but which no one would choose to enter who prefers to rest his life on facts however few, to fancies however inviting.

It is to explain and relieve, if possible, the state of soul represented by these words, that we would write. To others we will leave the task of meeting argument by argument, and of counteracting negation by affirmation. For ourselves our aim will be to analyze this state of mind by comparing it with an emotional state well known to Catholic directors by the name of "scruples." Then, having considered doubt in its nature, it will be natural to examine into its causes. Lastly, some principles may be laid down for its cure.

Scruples are a disease of the conscience. Just as there are lax consciences which override almost every regula-

tion of law, so are there timorous, scrupulous consciences
which press law till it becomes unbearable. Strictly speaking, if conscience is a dictate of right reason, scrupulousness is but the distorted shadow of conscience.

Though it is not always easy at first sight to say what is
a scrupulous and what a sensitive conscience, a little experience, aided by the principles of ascetic theology, will
in the end make the matter certain. Of course, experience
is worth more than theory, because no general theoretical
diagnosis will meet individual cases. One of the most common symptoms of a scrupulous conscience is an impossibility of making use of reflex principles. The moral theologian knows that the judicious use of these principles is
the very life of a true healthy spirituality. Such moral
principles as "Where there is doubt there is liberty," or
"Positive law does not bind us under grave inconven-
ience," or "Possession is nine points of the law," or "There
is no sinning through ignorance, save when ignorance is a
sin," serve to raise the dead letter of ethics into a living
guide of conscience. Even the extremely delicate virtue of
ἐπιείκεια, whereby the letter of law must be sacrificed to
the spirit, has an important function in practical matters.
But it is just in these matters that the timid soul will take
fright. Every application of a reflex principle that enlarges
liberty or lessens obligation appears an act of disloyalty to
conscience.

It is not that the mind is unable to agree that reflex
principles have a legitimate place in questions of conduct.
Such souls often possess a rare hold of abstract ethics, if
they happen to be professors of moral theology. They
have often the power of discussion, but not of use. They
will agree that reflex principles are loyal, pertinent, necessary. They will even consent that in the case in point such

principles could lawfully be employed. But they will not employ them. Sometimes gifted with a strong power of drawing up an ethical argument, they stop short of drawing a practical conclusion. In extreme cases they will conclude, "This should be done"; but they will leave it undone. In scholastic language they may have a firm will to reach the end (*voluntas*), and an equally firm will to take the means (*intentio*), but through some moral paralysis they cannot actually will to act (*imperium*).

The same want of determination is found not merely in this sphere of volition, but in the intellectual sphere. It is not uncommon to find minds that are competent, and even highly competent, in drawing up arguments which they have no power of completing by their necessary conclusions. Through some fault of mind they cannot keep purely intellectual concepts in focus. As all ratiocination is the recognition of the fact as standing under the law, and of the phenomenon as related to the substance, they seem incapable of keeping these two concepts upon a plane that would enable them to make the necessary comparison and draw the necessary conclusion. When engaged in examining the fact, the principle or law fades into a mere useless reminiscence; when the principle or law is presented to consciousness, the fact becomes a mere uneventful incident. Thus there are many minds who would be surprised and even offended if their hold on the great principle of causality was doubted. They will maintain, and even make a good show of proving, the omnipresence of this great causal law. Though to them the whole universe is a unity because of this law, they take fright as soon as it is suggested that there is a first cause. To their minds such an uncaused being would be the denial of their first principle, when in reality he would only be the justification of it. Nor can they reject him merely on these grounds unless they equally reject the law itself, which is confessedly an uncaused concept, if not indeed an uncaused reality.

In the same way, much of the difficulty created by the subject of evil is due to an inability to draw conclusions after drawing up premises. To many minds the existence of evil remains an irrefutable argument against the existence of God, seeing that God is not God if He is not good. Now the doctrine of the existence of a personal first cause who has a character is not merely the rationalization of the problem of evil, but the destruction of it. Whether there is a God or not, evil exists; and its existence must remain a difficulty in all attempts to bring all things and events under the law of causality. To assert that God exists is but to assert that evil does come under the law of causality, and that it is only permitted by a good God to serve a good purpose. Instead of the existence of God throwing the existence of evil into a more painful shadow, it serves to rob it of much of its darkness by showing that evil itself falls under law and turns to good by the will and wisdom of the first good. That there are minds—honest yet scrupulous minds—who find it impossible to reconcile supreme goodness with evil is due to their powerlessness to allow arguments to develop their rightful conclusions, in spite of the difficulties which beset all truths, especially the highest.

A second characteristic of scrupulous souls is their inability to piece together circumstantial arguments. It is sometimes thought that circumstantial, or what has been called convergent, evidence is not such as can justify certitude; but this is a false opinion. In truth, the only means of proving facts is convergent evidence. This must not be taken as a denial that such a fact as "This person whom I see is Caius" is not an object of intuition. Assuredly it is an object of intuition; but if we begin to examine the evidence for it, we shall see that it is circumstantial and convergent in nature. Thus, if we say that we know that the person nearing us is Caius because of his height, this should prove nothing, seeing that there are probably millions of this height. Take his size, voice, hair, eyes, features, walk, manner—there are probably millions that share with him these qualities. Taken individually, then, these qualities prove nothing, and would identify no one. Taken together, joined in one individual, they denote Caius, and no one else. They are the stroke of the brush, the light and shadow, the line and curve, the form and colour, needed to make Caius something more than the *individuum vagum,* or "rational animal," of anthropology.

In matters of duty there are many who have not the power of putting matters together, or of summing up. They can see one thing and see it clearly. But their minds refuse to take a general view which includes all the circumstances. If they take what they call a general view, it is by leaving out most of the circumstances which particularize the object. Only the specific, not the individual, qualities are retained in consciousness and conscience. Such consciences are unable to formulate the law or the exception to the law which applies to the case. Thus, for example, there are some who through a scruple would leave a relation in grave sickness in order to go to Mass on Sunday. It is true that the letter of the law obliges each one to hear Mass. But the law of Sunday Mass is now in conflict with the law of charity. Moreover, the full circumstances are, that there is some one in a dangerous state, with no one to see them, and that Sunday Mass is a positive obligation, and so on. The timid conscience cannot sum up all the circumstances, individualizing the case in point and removing it, not indeed beyond the jurisdiction of law, but beyond the jurisdiction of the law of Sunday Mass, and placing it under the law of charity. Were we asked whether such scrupulosity of conscience is common, we should be inclined to answer that in our experience it is less common than the scrupulous impossibility of drawing a conclusion; and, certainly, less common in matters of conscience than in matters of thought.

Indeed, it is in matters of thought that this particular kind of scrupulosity has widest rule. Far from being easy to observe the particular, it is very difficult. If experience teaches us anything, it is how rare it is to find a full and accurate description of even the simplest experience. No two descriptions of the same phenomenon, no two statements of the same event, ever agree. It may be said that men may not agree in describing this or that accident of the substance, even when they do agree with regard to the substance. But it must be borne in mind that what is accidental to the species is, so to say, essential to the individual. As the scholastics would say, *"Haec ossa et hoc corpus"* do not belong to the species. But they constitute Caius, Sempronius, and the individual man. Without them, all ideas are but a logarithm of the reality. It is being increasingly felt, and idealists are causing it to be remembered, that the so-called physical sciences do not deal with concrete things, but with abstractions. Acoustics, heat, electricity, mechanics, dynamics, biology, and all other positive sciences do not deal with the individual as such, but with such abstractions as sound, heat, electricity, local motion, material energy, and life. None of these is confessedly occupied with the concrete, but with the abstract. There is still needed a science of the individual, just as in a workshop, with its frame-benders, plate-layers, riveters, caulkers, enamellers, brass-workers, blacksmiths, there are the fitters who take the various disjointed materials and piece them into a unity.

Now it is quite conceivable that one man might unite in himself the craft of all those we have enumerated, and yet have no turn for fitting together; and we can conceive a workman with a genius for fitting, who could make no headway with brass-finishing or riveting. In the same way, we may see how a man may possess a general knowledge of all the abstractions embraced under mathematics, logic, physical science, and biology, and yet have no head for unifying and therefore individualizing these sciences into a further science. This is but to assert the difference between mere knowledge in general, or general knowledge and philosophy. Were we to exemplify this, we should say that although Butler had no very general knowledge, he was a philosopher; and Herbert Spencer was not a philosopher, though he had an extraordinarily general knowledge.

All this will lead us to recognize that there are numbers of minds so constituted that they cannot take a general view of things without burying themselves in abstractions, and losing hold of the individual phenomenon or event. We may exemplify them by such an event as the resurrection of Jesus Christ. They may make the sincerest professions of want of prejudice, which merely means that they will conscientiously weigh out some measure of toleration to their opponents' arguments, but none to their opponents' conclusion. Then they will proceed to reckon up the phenomenon: an empty tomb—a few soldiers, the basest of men, and the most superstitious—dazed by an earth-

quake—drowsy after a long night watch; a group of en-
thusiasts—hypnotized by a mystic prophecy—stunned by
their own flagrant denial—goaded by repentance—dis-
couraged by their leader's death—longing to find their
leader not dead but living; and the case is judged. They
have not summed up the phenomenon. That they could
not do; that, indeed, no one could do. But they have made
abstraction from the various circumstances that could
mark the phenomenon itself with its stamp of individuality. They make no mention, or lay no stress on the character of Jesus: his sublime doctrine—his clear prophecy—
the character of the disciples—of Peter, John, Andrew,
Thomas, and the others—of the appearances to men—to
fishermen, i.e., to men who are not easily frightened—
in broad daylight—on the shore—in a closed room; to
men who doubted, to men who had everything to lose by
believing; to a few, to many, now here, now there; to men
who laid down their lives for the truth of this event; to
men whose preaching of this event has been the resurrection of a fallen world.

These and other accidental circumstances give the
event its unique character, marking it off from all else;
and are at once its individuality and its defence. But it is
not easy for all minds, and it is perhaps especially hard
for merely logical minds, to take this broad, philosophic,
and therefore individual and accurate view of the event.
They will view it as an episode in cosmic evolution, or as
an incident in ethics, or as an event in history, or as related to the law of causality, or as a phenomenon of anthropology, or as the outcome of a tribal longing, or as
matter for psychical investigation, or as evidence of hallu-
cination, or as extremely interesting to students of mysticism. That is, they will take up an abstract standpoint;

they will try to weigh the most momentous event in the world by the baby balance of some one science. And they will scruple to accredit it with any supernatural import merely because their balance, true to its limitations, reports this phenomenon to be substantially the same as every other phenomenon which it has the power to weigh. Minds that find in such a judgment the duty of not moving forward to the whole of the phenomenon may well be said to be suffering from an intellectual scruple.

We have been hitherto engaged in making a parallel between the scruple of duty and the scruple of doubt—i.e., between moral and intellectual scruples. We may close this first part of our Conference by remarking that women by their temperament are more prone to moral scruples, and men to intellectual scruples. This is the general psychological law, which has its necessary exceptions. When these exceptions take place they are generally remarkable. Women, as a rule, are not sceptics; nor are men devotees. But if there is a sadder sight than a man given over to scruples, it is that of a woman who has thrown over belief.

Moreover, a common trait of the morally and intellectually scrupulous is their power of argument, which we have agreed not to accept as evidence of any great power of reasoning, or at least of thought. Wise directors of souls know how many subtle and seemingly irrefutable arguments scrupulous consciences can bring up to prove their point. They will dispute a point of law or fact with all the subtlety of a dialectician. Yet all the while their one defect is a want of common sense to enable them to see things and events exactly as they are, and not as they present themselves to their scrupulous conscience. But this subtle power of argument and this strange paralysis of the will power or of the reason are by no means allowed to dominate their heart and mind. Souls are rarely found to be scrupulous in every department of duty or thought. They contrive to make occult compensation for over-strictness in one point by over-laxity in another. Souls that are scrupulous about their attention at prayers may have no scruple about tale-bearing or uncharitableness. Men who stretch the claims of argument to breaking point in the matter of the divinity of Jesus Christ, may make no scruple in accepting the whole doctrine or evolution or totemism, or the persistence of force. Indeed, the likelihood is that in less rational departments of thought they fall into the superstitions of science. To the theological mind few things are more instructive than the interest shown nowadays in spiritualism by scientists of the front rank, whose devotion to reason prevents them recognizing to the full the claims of faith. It is their peculiar method of making occult compensation for their slighted instincts.

We may now turn from the nature of this scruple of doubt to an examination of its causes. We are not concerned to inquire how far this depends on external circumstances. When speaking of the problem of faith we may have suggested that the extreme form of doubt which has now become an epidemic of our epoch, has its roots in the racial characteristics of western peoples. But to trace the extent to which climate, locality, and other external forces create a psychological atmosphere is not our intention here.

Every inquiry into the origin of intellectual scrupulousness must begin with a recognition of the great, and indeed dominant, part played by the imagination. Not only does imagination usurp the place of reason, but it masquerades as the very power it has ousted. Much of the evil is due to our education, which is concerned with words and aspects rather than with things and with thinking. The insistence upon mathematical sciences has not a little to do with begetting an unruly imagination, seeing that mathematics deal chiefly with abstract quantity which appeals to the visual imagination, even under its most abstruse form of algebraic and trigonometrical formulae. Plato's view, that good mathematicians make bad philosophers, is well known. He was but expressing the truth that the extreme accuracy of the mathematical sciences unfits the mind for broad balanced views. Who would ever expect to work out a difficult problem in algebra by making allowances for the working out, or by approaching it with an unbiased mind, or by being alive to convergent probabilities, or by giving some place to rational authority, or by viewing things on the whole, or by leaving an opening for exceptions? These, indeed, are the very nerves of all philosophic thought. Yet to suggest them to a mathematician is but to raise a smile, so far removed is the mere working out of quantitative relations removed from real thought.

This leads us at once to another cause of doubt, viz., want of true thought. It is not easy at first blush to say what reasoning is or is not. According to our definition, we might be obliged to say that doubt was now due to too much, and now to too little reasoning. Men who have acquired a mathematical facility for supplying premisses for any conclusion, and for drawing conclusions from premisses, through Barbara, Celarent, and other syllogistic forms, may engender doubts from their fatal facility. Conclusions or premisses fostering unbelief may be suggested to their minds in youth or middle age. It appears to them an act of disloyalty to their understanding to think that such arguments could ever jeopardise their allegiance to the truth. Soon, perhaps, they form a complete syllogistic expression of the argument. This remains in their mind, and crops up unbidden at all times. So accustomed do they become to the whole chain of argument, and so deft at "running it through," so to say, from beginning to end, that no matter where they find themselves set down in it, they can run it up and down almost automatically, until they think it has become a part of their being—when in reality it can hardly be looked upon as part of their thought. But it is clear that this habit of argument-making may easily dispose the mind to doubt; and according as a man holds or does not hold that this is true reasoning, so will he maintain or deny that the scruple of his doubt has been begotten of sound reasoning.

We should be shirking an important part of our examination did we not inquire whether doubt may not have a moral cause. In the case of the morally scrupulous it is not permitted to deny that their scruples often betray faults much more grave than those they scruple to commit. Thus they are almost always wanting in obedience; and they are not seldom proud. When their disobedience springs from pride they are practically incurable. Thus they will feel no scruple in paying little attention to the formal commands of their director. Nor will they lack arguments to support them in their disobedience. They will make little of the opinions of one who is a specialist in moral matters. With no very great experience they will disagree with an outside unbiased opinion, and headstrongly undertake that most difficult of all works—the cure of their own ailments. In intellectual matters we should be giving unfaithful witness if we did not draw attention to the same possibility of moral causes. It is not for us, nor, indeed, for every one, to say whether in this case or that doubt has its roots in some moral defect. We are merely making an examination of the malady in general, which would be far from complete if we denied that doubt could be very vitally connected with disobedience and pride, i.e., with a feeble recognition of the authority of others, and a strong recognition of our own.

We may now be prepared to outline the cure of doubt. Briefly, to remove the cause is to remove the effect. In the first place, a thorough diagnosis of the doubt must be made. It is clear that the person least fitted to pronounce judgment is the patient. He alone can state symptoms. But he alone is peculiarly unfitted to draw conclusions. The matter must be entrusted to another. One of the most obvious remedies in extreme cases is a change of scene. Whilst minds dwell in the same place and daily meet the same circumstances, interests, duties, ideas, their mind will continue in the same round of thought. Hence the oft-quoted remedy of a sea voyage. Newman's voyage in the Mediterranean began the Oxford Movement; his retreat from Oxford to the poverty and silence of Littlemore ended with his submission to the Holy See. Or to take a case which may come home even more forcibly to us here today. Romanes the agnostic became Romanes the believer through taking up his abode under this roof, where he came into touch with the ten thousand spiritual forces of this city, lent as a lesson by ages of faith to an age of doubt. And if change of scene cannot be had, how often do wise guides bid men give over reading and arguing and take to prayer. Was this in Browning's mind when he wrote of "The Guardian Angel of Fano"?

> I would rest
> My head beneath thine, whilst thy healing hands
> Close-covered both my eyes beside thy breast;

Pressing the brain, which too much thought expands,
Back to its proper size again, and smoothing
Distortion down till every nerve had soothing,
And all lay quiet, happy, and suppressed.

A further remedy is in the hard-earned control of the imagination. As the imagination is a power for evil it is equally a power for good. It must not be allowed to be a master, as it makes a bad master but a good servant. Where it has really no place it should never be allowed to usurp a place. The higher mysteries of God are just those in which the imagination fails to reach the full truth. We should resolutely instruct the imagination that such a doctrine as the eternal three in one is beyond its grasp, that the trinity in unity which the mystery contains is beyond mathematics and therefore beyond the imagination.

Lastly, the scruple of doubt can yield only to an earnest and lasting discipline of the will.

(*Faith and Prayer*)

HINDRANCES TO PRAYER

〰〰〰

TO REALIZE the true character of the relations in which distractions and pride stand to prayer, we must first know the effects of prayer. Theology informs us that these effects are four, viz., merit, impetration, satisfaction, pleasure.[1] For the first three intention and not attention is necessary; for the last attention must be added to intention. It does not require much thought to make this clear to us. Merit is an increase of grace resulting from an exercise of charity. Where there is not even an implicit intention of doing our actions through love of God there can be no merit. Impetration is the power of obtaining what we ask. Though this does not always require charity, it always requires an intention of seeking our favour from God. So too, satisfaction or the power of blotting out temporal punishment which is attached to the afflictive or penitential aspect of prayer, can only be brought about by the intention of bearing pain for the love of God.

In all these cases it is evident that actual attention is not necessary. Whilst the initial intention lasts, or in other words, whilst the initial intention is unrecalled, our prayers are meritorious, impetratory, and satisfactory. But if we wish prayer to be a pleasure we must pay attention to what we are saying. Intention is an act of the will whereby we refer our action to God. Attention is an act of the mind whereby we make ourselves vividly conscious

[1] Delectatio: a scholastic word difficult to translate. It might be rendered as "spiritual joy."

of the objects of sensation or thought. It is at once evident that of the two, intention is much more important than attention, though this is not always recognized. It is a common characteristic of heresy to lay more stress on attention and the outward decorum of vocal prayer than on the inward intention which gives it birth. Yet because we remark this we must not be taken to discredit attention, which to some modern psychologists seems the essential act of human intelligence. It is worth noting that they also detect in it a certain influx of the will which directs the mind to one object rather than to others. This affective element in attention allies it with prayer.

Theologians are responsible for a very useful division of attention. With St. Thomas they note that whilst praying we may attend to the words we say—or to the meaning of the words we say—or to the "end" of the words we say, i.e., to God. To attend to God in prayer, even if the sense of the words is forgotten, is to be fervent in prayer. It is, indeed, good to be busy about the mere mechanical pronunciation of the words—and better to attend to their meaning—but best of all to unite our minds with God who is the goal of all prayer. This is the wise teaching of St. Thomas and should hinder us from judging ourselves to have prayed ill, merely because we have overlooked the perfect enunciation of words in the fervour of our union with God. It is notorious that vocal prayers are sometimes, if not often, said with slovenliness in Catholic congregations. Without wishing altogether to excuse what is not altogether excusable, I would suggest that part of the seeming slovenliness may be due to the stress laid upon the higher kind of attention.

But where there is no attention even of the lowest and most mechanical kind there can be little or no pleasure in prayer. Distractions kill the joy of praying. Few mental pains exceed that of being obliged to repeat words which are repugnant to the ideas we wish to keep in consciousness. For example, to be forced to read light literature in a time of deep grief is agony of soul. If the soul is teased with pleasing distractions—and our distractions are very nearly related to our pleasures—the recitation of a prayer can be extremely burdensome. But attention soon begets pleasure. Even in spiritual matters the proverb *Age quod agis* is the secret of successful prayer, because the secret of joyful prayer. In common vocal prayer it is wonderful how much joy can be found in attention to the right saying or chanting of the common psalm or hymn. I dare say we have all experienced a thrill of pleasure in taking part in a united singing, say, of the *Veni Creator Spiritus* or of the *Te Deum*—or even of the simple Litany we sing at Benediction. But it is a pleasure attendant only on attention. Distractions may banish it in a moment. To those of us who have been present or who have taken part in a great function of the Church, say, an ordination, the meaning not merely of the many vocal prayers, but of the bodily prayers, the bowings, genuflexions, and the rest, afford one of the keenest of spiritual pleasures. Especially is this the case if by God's grace we are able to raise our mind beyond that which is outward and feast our eye on another throne-room and on another, heavenly, ceremonial.

It is hardly necessary to say what distractions are; most of us, I dare say, have something more than an academic acquaintance with them. Distractions are thoughts which may or may not be permissible at other times, but are not permissible during prayer. The chief injury they do is to withdraw the attention of the mind from the words—or from the meaning of the words—or from the thought of God. They need not be bad nor even idle thoughts. At other times and in other circumstances to think of them may be a duty. But it is wrong to allow them to fill the time of prayer. They must be kept like catechumens in the approaches of our soul and not allowed into the Holy of Holies. They arise chiefly from our occupation or our affections. Let a man tell his distractions, and he has laid bare his affections. Where a man's treasure is there is his heart.

There is a curious visual phenomenon known as "after-images." If we look steadily at a brightly coloured object and then either shut our eyes or turn them towards a white surface the coloured object will reappear. Nor will it have its own natural colours; it will be clad in what are called complementary colours. Somewhat in the same way, if our minds are much thrown among engaging or absorbing objects, we cannot suddenly direct our thoughts towards holy things without finding ourselves distracted by a hundred teasing after-images mirrored on the background of our prayers. St. Thomas More puts the matter forcibly if a little quaintly: "But when men are wealthy and well at their ease, while our tongue pattereth upon our prayers apace, good God! how many mad ways our mind wandereth awhile!" [1] And it often happens that the false colours of the after-image are more fascinating than the reality itself. The important matter is to avoid distractions as far as we may be able. Rules for this are easily given; but it is the practice rather than the remembrance of rules that clears the soul of those "dead flies" that "spoil the sweetness of the ointment." [2]

[1] *A Dialogue of Comfort* (London, 1847), ch. xix, p. 68.
[2] Eccles. 10:1.

It is evident that if our occupations and our affections are the chief sources of distractions our first rule will be to control our affections. It is useless to take in hand our distractions in prayer only during the time of prayer. Our greatest hope lies in fighting the enemy beyond our frontiers. If there are any occupations which without being necessary are very distracting, we must manfully put an end to them. It is said of one of our English Vicars Apostolic, Bishop Walmesly, that he was a devoted student of mathematics. However, on finding that his studies painfully distracted him at the altar he gave them up. I need not say that it is the spirit rather than the letter of this example which we suggest to you. Often to those who read much distractions come from what they need not, or should not, read. It is not unusual to give up certain kinds of reading before examinations lest they should prove too distracting.

In the same way a class of distractions arises from an abnormal absorption, for example, in mere romantic literature. It would be a miracle if there were no distractions awaiting those who spend two or three hours a day in novel-reading and never give half an hour to their Bible or their *Imitation,* or other kinds of spiritual reading. What a man sows he reaps. Let him sow distractions, and he will reap distractions. If, then, we are willingly given up to a course of action which provides a fruitful brood of distracting thoughts, our first rule must be to put an end to the cause. With most of us, however, distractions spring from our lawful occupations and, indeed, from our duties. To prevent these from oversowing the tares of distractions we must learn, more and more, to be in, yet not of, the world. We must neither add to nor subtract from our round of work; or if add and subtract we must, let us subtract all needless anxiety and only add fervour of intention. The household of St. Jane Frances de Chantal used to say, "Madame's first director made her pray only three times a day, and the whole household was upset. But His Lordship the Bishop of Geneva"—St. Francis of Sales—"makes her pray all day long, and she disturbs no one." She had been taught the lesson that the secret of true prayer is to "serve the Lord." A great step will have been taken when we have learnt to do all under the eye and for the honour of our master. We shall not do our duty whether of work or of prayer with less heart or with less success because we do it for him whose judgment is final and just. Then when the time of prayer comes we shall be the better able to tie up our anxieties, so to say, at the threshold of our soul. Or if they find an entrance into our prayers, we shall not weary ourselves in useless guerrilla warfare with them. We shall quietly renew our intention and make an act of heartfelt humility, thus turning the dart of our enemy into an arrow of fervent prayer.

A second rule for avoiding distractions is—by paying attention. If we cannot pay the highest and best kind of attention, let us make use of a lower or of the lowest. Or, if we are distracted whilst employing the lower kind of attention, it may be God's gracious way of suggesting a higher. Never give up the struggle, which will end only with life. But above all, never give up under a sense of depression.

Our chief enemy is the imagination. But we should remember that unless our will gives way, the imagination, even if it is a source of annoyance, is not a source of sin; and though it may rob prayer of its sweetness, it need not rob it of its merit, its impetration, and its satisfaction.

More consoling and sensible words I cannot find than those of the great mystic St. Teresa. In speaking of the relief she felt when first taught the difference between the imagination and the understanding, she remarks that many do not grasp the difference; and "hence arise the afflictions of many who are given to prayer (at least this happens to persons who are not learned); hence also arise melancholies and loss of health and a total neglect of prayer, through not considering that there is an interior world. And as we cannot prevent the heavenly bodies from going on in their rapid course, so neither can we stop the wanderings of the imagination." "When I see souls so very careful about being attentive at their prayers, and about understanding them also, so that it seems they dare not so much as stir or divert their thoughts lest they should lose the little pleasure and devotion they feel in their prayer, I then clearly discover how little they understand." "We must remember that the business does not consist in thinking but in loving much; do, therefore whatever may excite you most to love. Perhaps we do not know what love is; it consists not in having greater delights, but greater resolutions and desires of pleasing God in everything and in endeavouring as far as possible not to offend him, and in beseeching him that he would promote the honour and glory of his Son and extend the bounds of the Catholic Church. These are signs of love. Do not imagine that it consists in not thinking on anything else and that all is lost, if you have a few distractions!" [1]

Distractions are closely connected with the sin of turning to creatures, whereas pride is essentially the turning away from God. Hence distractions, though common

[1] *The Interior Castle* (London, 1859), pp. 76–117.

enough with men, are more naturally a besetting fault of the weaker sex, in whom the emotions and the imagination normally reach a higher state of development. Hence though some of the remarks I have made may probably have seemed exaggerated, a spiritual director with even a limited experience would no doubt look upon them as justified by feminine psychology. Men are naturally more inclined to keep from prayer through pride than to give it up through distractions. And of the two hindrances to prayer it is evident that pride is the more dangerous and the harder to cure.

We have already seen that the acknowledgment of God's excellence is an essential part of prayer. Pride, far from being the acknowledgment of God's excellence and infinity, is the undue seeking after our own excellence. It is the most formal turning away from God, and when added to other sins it adds to their guilt. If we are to believe St. Thomas, our first parents sinned through pride, not so much in desiring to be like God, as in desiring the divine likeness without the acceptance and the acknowledgment of the divine help. The proud man thinks he can stand alone. Consequently the proud man cannot pray. He does not feel the need of external help. He is sufficient for himself. His pride will often keep him from ignobler sins; it is a tyrant that cannot brook a division of its autocracy. It can reign equally over good works and evil, because, though it cannot make evil good, it can make good works evil. It is never so dangerous as when it is reigning alone. And as men given over to irrational scepticism can only be convinced by a *demonstratio ad absurdum* or by an *argumentum ad hominem,* so pride can rarely be driven out of a soul until God has allowed it to fall into some lesser but more degrading sin. It is commoner with men than with women, for the reason that men, being naturally the stronger, are naturally drawn to trust in their own strength. It is often noted that women are more devoted church-goers than men, and that as a rule their confessions are less brief and businesslike. Men are more tempted to think prayer useless; but when they do pray, they are less likely to be vexed by distractions.

We remarked that distractions are opposed to attention, whereas pride is opposed to intention. To justify this we have only to recall the fact that intention is the deliberate seeking of means to an end; intention in prayer being the deliberate seeking from God of the means to reach our last end. It is at this that pride strikes. As it glories in its own acquirements and seeks its own end by itself, the whole fabric of prayer appears foolish, or at least childish, to it. It finds it hard to go on its knees. It finds it harder to say "Our Father." It thinks that to be childlike is to be childish. It cannot see the force of our blessed Lord's words, "Amen, I say to you, whosoever shall not receive the Kingdom of God as a little child, shall not enter into it." [1] It does not realise that since the Kingdom of God must be received, it must also be sought. It can do much good. But it cannot acknowledge from whom the good came, and who must bless it unto its increase.

Pride, in laying the axe to the root of intention, paralyses the possibility of prayer. Distractions suspend some of the more pleasurable functions of prayer, but pride makes prayer an impossibility, because an absurdity. An example of this is painted by no other than our blessed Lord himself, and, as we might expect, it is recorded by St. Luke, the Evangelist of prayer. There is little need to

[1] Mark 10:15.

dwell at length on the classical parable of the Pharisee
and the Publican. The Pharisee is a type of the proud; the
Publican of the humble. It was to be expected that
"prayer of him that humbleth himself shall pierce the
clouds." [1] The character of the Pharisee is sketched with
great fulness and truth. He could apparently defend himself against the crimes of usury, fraud, and adultery. He
was careful about the laws of fasting and almsdeeds. He
obeyed the commandments and performed the works of
satisfaction. Outwardly he was an exemplary member of
the community; but there his goodness ended. He was one
of those "whited sepulchres which outwardly appear to
men beautiful, but within are full of dead men's bones and
of all filthiness." [2] Pride had corrupted all his good deeds.
He belonged to those "who trusted in themselves as just
and despised others." [3] His pride has merited the fine
epigram of the poet—

> Two went to pray. Or rather say
> One went to brag, th' other to pray.
> One stands up close and treads on high,
> Where th' other dares not send his eye.
> One nearer to God's altar trod;
> The other to the altar's God. [4]

The Pharisee did not altogether forget the duties of his
position and what was expected of him. The holy name is
invoked. He even "gives thanks" to God for what he is.
But he contrives to corrupt these outwardly good things
by the loathsome spirit of pride. His thanksgiving is only
lip-deep. All the while he is trusting in himself as just.
Moreover his words are as unlike a prayer as they could

[1] Ecclus. 35:21.
[2] Matt. 23:27.
[3] Luke 18:9.
[4] Crashaw, *Steps to the Temple*.

well be. Man is never so contemptible as when he is boasting. A braggart cuts a sorry figure at all times, but especially before the Court of Heaven. Nothing is more painful than to witness the folly of those who think that the
heavenly ranks are fixing their eyes with wonder upon
them; as if their goodness were drawing from God the
words, "Hast thou considered my servant Job, that there
is none like him in the earth." [1] The Pharisee was one of
those who made a show of prayer only as an opportunity
of displaying the spiritual wares of his soul and of saying,
"I am rich and made wealthy, and have need of nothing,"
at the same time that God was saying, "Thou knowest not
that thou art wretched, and miserable, and poor, and
blind, and naked. I counsel thee to buy of me gold fire-
tried that thou mayest be made rich, and mayest be
clothed in white garments, and that the shame of thy
nakedness may not appear; and anoint thine eyes with
eye-salve that thou mayest see." [2]

If the Pharisee had only kept to a verse of the penitential psalms he might have prayed to some purpose. But
whatever his reasons, he seems to have preferred his own
prayer. It may have been composed in more fashionable
Hebrew. But, in truth, he was not a success as a com-
poser. For whilst doing his best to make a prayer, he
merely succeeded in making a speech—which is the least
successful way of approaching the infinite. Nothing can
be more painful than the accurately drawn figure of this
exemplary member of the synagogue standing near the
altar making his virtues the subject matter of a speech,
then going down self-satisfied that he had made a very
creditable show before Jehovah, and little suspecting the

[1] Job 1:8.
[2] Apoc. 3:17–18.

true value set upon his boasting by the wise and good God.

The figure of the Publican is drawn with equal skill. He stands out before us as an engaging type of those lowly and self-depreciatory souls who win every one to their side. He is utterly unconscious of all else but his own sin. Though the figure of the braggart blocked the view of the altar, he does not see him, or he does not notice him. The sight of the Pharisee's self-satisfaction was calculated more than anything else to distract him from himself. How often do we hear men say, "I will never set my foot in church whilst such a one is there"; or, "I am wicked, but I am not a hypocrite." The Publican, sorely tempted as he may have been to mingle comparisons with his prayers, kept undauntedly to himself. The Pharisee compared himself with the Publican, with what success we know. But to the Publican nothing was present but God and his sin—God's mercifulness, capable of saving him, and his misery craving to be saved. His prayer, if not taken from the liturgy of the chosen people, was full of the spirit of true liturgical prayer. He based his hopes, not on the realization of his own strength, but on his sense of sin and on his own realization of God's mercy towards sinners. And thus, whereas the Pharisee made the longer prayer, the Publican made the better; for he who had wrought many good deeds spoiled them by pride, and he who had wrought many bad deeds blotted them out by humility.

We endeavoured to lay down some simpler rules for the lessening or for the management of our distractions. To provide rules for the lessening of pride is a harder task. Pride is a vice royal. It aims at reigning in the soul. Nor when once it has set up its throne can it be deposed by anything but its rival virtue, humility. We cannot oust it by any stratagem. It yields only to a direct attack. The one advice worth giving to a proud man is that which he is least likely to welcome. We can but say, "Be humble. God is your father. Kneel at his feet and own yourself his child." It is not the most reassuring, but it is the only policy towards pride. Nowadays it is safe to say that pride is a besetting sin of the world. Perhaps it has always borne its present supremacy. We cannot tell. But whilst it is useless to make comparisons between the times that are and that have been, it is impossible to close our eyes to the pride that still swells throughout the world. I know not which of the two—whether pride or humility—has the larger following. It is enough to know that the "pride of life" is still a master-vice, indeed a tyrant-vice, reigning over a wide jurisdiction. Our Father who is in Heaven is everywhere acknowledged—and denied; adored—and scouted; loved—and ignored. It is not easy to reconcile all this denial of God with the self-denial which is the soul of true humility.

Perhaps pride, like the sea, has its ebb and flow, its low and high tide. If this be so, the state of God's interests in the world of today is hard to sum up. Pride would seem to be in flood when men in great part have given up prayer; when many "houses of prayer" have come to be looked upon and used as mere meeting-places; when the preacher's pulpit has been degraded to the rostrum of political agitators; when men come to church not to cry mercy to God, but to while away a pleasant hour of the idle day of the week. Yet this judgment of the world may be as untrue as it is dispiriting. It may be truer, as it is more consoling to think, that if pride and forgetfulness of God are at their flood, signs are not wanting that the

waters are beginning to subside. When prayer is coming
to be looked upon as a duty; when the old liturgical services of the Church have not merely their apologists but
their admirers; when social wounds are acknowledged to
be beyond the reach of statistics and legislation; when the
Creator is being gradually reinstated as the first phenomenon and first cause of creation, pessimism may well
be thought superfluous.

However this may be, it is best for us to look away from
the world outside us to the world within. In our lives the
years when pride was strongest were those when, not altogether through neglect but more through distaste, the
simple duty of standing under the divine eye morning and
evening became a burden. There are few of us perhaps
who may be privileged to go through life without days of
painful severance and misunderstanding with God due to
the strength and the headstrongness of our will. The severance will last, and the misunderstanding will remain
unhealed, until in childlike self-forgetfulness we begin
afresh that prayer of the lowly which pierces the clouds
and brings down God's strength and peace into our souls.
If by God's mercy the day of estrangement from him is
not yet come, may he keep it ever from us! Whilst we are
still in the stress of the struggle with our soul's foes, we
hardly know that we stand, and we know not when we
may fall. Our souls will be ours only if we watch and pray.
And as we know not what nor how to ask, our lifelong
prayer must ever be, "Lord, teach us to pray."

(*Faith and Prayer*)

Retreat Conferences

MORNING PRAYER

〽〽〽〽〽

Luke 11:1,2. And it came to pass that as He was in a certain place praying, when He ceased, one of His disciples said to Him: Lord, teach us to pray, as John also taught his disciples.

And He said to them, When you pray, say: Father, hallowed be Thy Name.

SOMEONE might see in this, the shorter form of the "Our Father," a sign of the great authority of St. Peter. A slightly longer form comes to us through the authority of the Apostle, St. Matthew; and someone of equal authority, or greater, would be needed even to suggest a shorter form. We may just meditate on the circumstances which we have detailed for us here.

St. Matthew's form comes in that great group of principles called the Sermon on the Mount. I think it is shown in St. Luke in its chronological position. The authority of St. Peter is now showing us that it was on the way up to Jerusalem. They were struck with our blessed Lord's prayer. They came upon Him, evidently in the morning, and they were very much struck by that. The Sacred Humanity was passing nights in prayer. We never have any details about those nights of prayer. St. Luke calls them "the Prayer of God." That is a mystery of mysteries, the prayer of the Son to the Father.

I venture to suggest there is no soul in which the present problem is not the problem of prayer, no soul that

155

could not be benefited by some more perfect way of praying. If it was true prayer it would have its effects in every department of our being—of our own individual life and of our own social life. The world is suffering now because prayer is no longer duly valued.

We see that our dear Lord spent the night in prayer. It does not mean every night; but He rose up early in order that He might give time to prayer. I often wonder whether certain lives could not be arranged on a wiser and more wholesome basis if they arranged things so that they had time for prayer. People are now so bewildered that they have to deceive themselves by putting the clock back. I never thought I should live to see that! In the great life out with God on the land, they never had anything to change. Elsewhere they are bewildered. They do not know what to do. The sun is not very much affected by Mr. Willett; even the beasts do not follow us. We are much more wise when we follow them. There are no ways of hastening cows. You shouldn't try to hasten cows! When we come back to simple things, we seem to be going more slowly. The cowman walks behind the cows, often whistling. Motors come and motors go. The cows walk steadily on. You can't hurry up nature, except by forcing things.

The morning hour is the one we have to arrange. We have stolen so much into the night, we have now to play a trick upon ourselves. What would you say of several nations cutting pieces off the front of the day and sewing them on at the end?

Nearly all religious communities are early risers. Our dear Lord, then, used to get up early to pray. I think that is a principle. Unfortunately, if a priest looks after any souls who desire to get up early, very often he has to prevent them. Many occupations nowadays do not wake up until nine o'clock at night, when one ought to be going to rest. It is terrible. A priest who has to guide certain souls does not know what to do. "Give us this night our nightly sleep" is very often more important for souls than daily bread. A good deal of hysteria among pious Catholics is owing to lack of sleep. They are very anxious to have morning prayer, but they do not get enough sleep, and their prayers suffer.

If life is ordered for the primary things, life becomes very simple and effective. One of the important things is morning prayer. It is even of great value for the body. If every morning people had a nice walk of a quarter of an hour and heard Mass, even if they did not say anything, but knelt there quite silently, like the candlesticks (candlesticks never make a noise, thank God!), it would be extraordinarily good for them. Some people have not sufficient intelligence to realise the physical effects of going out. Some do. I buried one of them the other day. It was a delight to see that dear soul tripping along to the seven o'clock Mass, even in wintertime. She was over eighty. People said, "Ah, yes,—but—!" They were dead and buried before she was! People sometimes shorten their lives by trying to prolong them. If they only neglected themselves a little, they would live longer.

The day should be so arranged that we get our prayer properly, just as we arrange to get our food properly. That appeals to our intelligence. Of all practical subjects, prayer is the most practical. Till people get their prayer settled, their life is not really settled. Prayer will be getting their life in order. Things must be in their proper place. Now, prayer must be in its place, and it must be given the chief place.

Hence, when we come to the "Our Father," it is like a spiritual horary. I imagine the one who asked Our Lord for it was St. Peter. That is why he does not put his name in. He asked Our Lord how to pray. Instantaneously, on the spur of the moment, He gave them a most methodical thing, as methodical as the multiplication table. The multiplication table is information in order. That is its advantage. No doubt St. Peter and the rest were quite astonished. There is nothing very striking in the prayer. It is not so beautiful as the prayers some people have composed. It is quite a short one. But everything is in it—everything that should be in any prayer. It contains all, in the proper order.

It is not only a prayer but a lesson. I imagine that a prayer that does not teach us something has just missed something.

Isn't it so delightful?—they talked about it. "Don't you think we had better ask Him something?—ask Him to teach us? Because we don't know how to pray. John the Baptist gave us some sort of prayer, but John isn't Jesus." So St. Peter said, "All right. I'll ask Him," and he said so simply, "Lord, teach us to pray."

How high we have soared when we really ask anybody to teach us! "Teach me." But to say that to God and really to mean it, is wonderful. It is extraordinary how much and how quickly we learn when we wish to be taught.

When we do not wish to be taught we overlook the obvious. The obvious becomes hidden. The Lord's Prayer is something that will go on teaching for the rest of our life.

You and I, when we were children, understood the "Our Father," but we did not understand it fully. We never shall. Even in eternity we shall never comprehend God, but we will understand Him more and more. So it is with this simple and fundamental prayer. Some occurrence in our spiritual life will suddenly make us say, "Now we understand, 'Thy Will be done.'"

The "Our Father" is an ordered series of human desires. It at once gets our desires into order. It gives us our end. What is more fundamental in our life than getting our desires in order? Very few desires in our life are wrong in themselves. It is only that they are out of place.

I can quite imagine this Sunday morning a number of Catholics have not been to Holy Mass. We could get a list of their various reasons. Some are on their holidays—so far from a church. "We couldn't really manage to get there." Yes. Well, in some families that would never occur. They always choose a place where there is Holy Mass. It is quite excellent to have a summer holiday, and take the children somewhere. That is splendid. There is nothing wrong in that. But when it interferes with Holy Mass for four Sundays or six, something is not in order. My parents certainly were of sufficient intelligence, that the first thing they would say was, "Where is the church?" They never did pretend to be pious parents. But they would have true scorn if you suggested a place fifteen miles from Mass—a fine bathing place for the children. My mother would probably have made some very direct remark for your intelligence. "Is there no place near a Catholic church where the children can bathe?"

Others are very tired and want to sleep. Sleep is a most excellent thing. People should sleep as long as they naturally can. Little children tell me they have missed the ten o'clock Mass because they were asleep. Imagine a poor child being asleep on a nice morning, at ten o'clock! A normal child is cock-crowing at six! If a child is asleep, it ought to be asleep. The desires of those parents to give the little ones sleep are not in the proper order. The sleep should have begun at six o'clock the evening before. If you say the modern town doesn't allow that, don't you think it would be a good thing to destroy the modern town?

We shall never get things right until we realise that the "Our Father" is the great litany of desires. When a desire is out of order, it defeats itself. Some people say they have missed Mass because they were up late at a ball. I never make the slightest commentary. If it doesn't strike them as comic, what can you do? The first lighting ground for the grace of God is human intelligence. When one has the need, and no desire, think of the plight into which that being has fallen. Death is the inevitable result.

Our dear Lord comes along and teaches us the great desires of the human heart. You and I must go quietly through them. When you listen to the Divine Office for forty or fifty years, you are struck by the frequent use of the "Our Father." That shows the Church's great concern that you should be teaching yourself, every day, to desire the right thing in the right order. In the religious life, you say that "Our Father" about ten times as often as persons in the world, until you are almost sick and tired of it. You say, "Here's another 'Our Father'!" Only after fifty years or so do you begin to realise the wisdom of Holy Mother the Church. Jesus Christ made that prayer. He is God. It may seem a very dry sort of prayer, but Jesus is God and He made it; and if we say it again and again we will see a great deal in it, and great deal by it. We shall see things against their proper background, in their proper perspective. Things that should not be in the foreground will not be there. Ends will not be degraded into means. No wonder it has been given the place of honour in the Divine Office.

Let us then just quietly think of the place of prayer in our life, and have it ordered for more perfect prayer. I never like people to think that their first resolution about prayer is to add something to their prayers. It is quite a common mistake of fervour to think it must add. Dear children in Jesus Christ, you must be extraordinarily careful about adding. The only thing you need add is a spiritual thing. We have to challenge the additions. If we have added so many things that we have not time to get through them, they become almost an insupportable burden. A little may be added, oh, yes. But it has to be challenged. It is easy to add something,—and very easy to subtract. If we add too much, we get such a distaste, we cannot go on. I am always frightened of speaking of prayer, lest people should think they must add something. But I do think in all our life there is room for a more perfect prayer, not more numerous. I dare say I should be better if I knocked off some of my prayers and did the others better—if they were less numerous but more perfect. If I were living my prayers instead of saying them, my life would be more perfect.

We should look again and again at the Lord's Prayer and see how simple it is. In the circumstances now teasing you and me, we should ask our dear Lord to teach us more and more of this prayer.

It was given by Him to teach us the way to Him.

(*The Craft of Prayer*)

PRAYER—HOW EASY IT IS

> Phil. 4:6. Be nothing solicitous; but in every thing by prayer and supplication, with thanksgiving, let your petitions be made known to God.

THAT is a passage of unparalleled beauty, and all the more moving to us who remember from what prison gloom it came.

Prayer is a most fascinating subject, having profound roots in human nature and in the Nature of God.

Prayer is one of the real occupations of our life. We are holy in so far as we pray. Our prayer is an index to our perfection and a means thereto. Indeed it is difficult to distinguish which is cause and which is effect.

Prayer is almost the easiest thing in the world. Our blessed Lord tells the Apostles they should pray always, therefore it must be easy. If our blessed Lord says we must pray always, it is no business of anybody's to set that aside. Prayer must be something extraordinarily easy—at least, some form of prayer. Movement is easy, but that does not mean that all forms of movement are easy. Some movements are so exceedingly difficult that they require great practice. In the same way, some forms of prayer are difficult not to do! But some are rather difficult physically for some people; other forms are psychologically or mentally difficult. It is difficult for those who do not know Latin very well to say the Divine Office, yet that is a very important form of prayer. Others can pray by thinking about God, and by doing that they get the habitual power of prayer. They can think about somebody if they love them. It is extraordinarily difficult for us not to think, if we love somebody.

Other forms of prayer are so divine as to be purely supernatural and extraordinary, given by God. We cannot merit them. We must not pray for them. Nothing could equal our blessed Lady's powers of prayer. Some were given to her by God. It was not the work of her will making them, though it was the work of her will accepting them. The giving was entirely extraordinary. It would not be right for anybody to try to desire such forms of prayer, or to set about acquiring them.

It is very consoling to think that it is difficult not to pray. Ordinary good Catholics are praying when they do not think they are. They are praying when they offer implicitly all that they are doing to God. The only thing we cannot offer to God and turn into a prayer is sin. If we could turn sin into a prayer, it would mean that we were turning away from sin. There is no detail of our life that cannot be made into a prayer. Ordinary people are constantly uniting their souls to God when they are scrubbing the floor—typewriting—doing things of no particular value. When they offer those things to God, they become of spiritual value. They are working because it is God's Will—and that makes their work into a prayer. That fundamental form of prayer can go on all day long. Other forms may be necessary. There is need of keeping in touch with God by kneeling down. Some sorts of prayer may consist in standing up or in sitting. But these bodily prayers could not be continuous. We cannot always be saying our morning prayers! Hence the great importance of following the Church, which has special times for special prayers. It maps out the day into prayer seven times a

day. There are two great times, morning and evening. It
prays at other special times. It makes that prayer into
bodily as well as vocal prayer. That continues for a very
considerable time. It may not bring any particular sensible
devotion. That does not matter. It is the collective prayer
of a group of Catholics externally worshipping God.

There is a form of prayer which goes on always, and
there are the good old-fashioned morning and night prayers. I do not think I could undertake the responsibility of
looking after a soul that was careless about morning and
night prayers. I only understand a "Garden of the Soul"
Catholic. It is a good old-fashioned thing to go down on
your knees. We worship God in that way.

If any form of prayer is of obligation, our first duty
would be to make that a real prayer. When we go to Mass
on Sunday, we should make that into a real prayer. Thank
God, when we go into a church where there are numbers
of poor people, we see real prayer. There is old Bridget in
the corner, asthmatical and can't hear; others are following the ritual in Latin or Greek; some are saying the
Rosary; others looking at the candlesticks; a mother is
looking after her baby,—perhaps she is praying best of
all. People ask me which is the best way of following
Mass. I think the best way is the way you want to;—but
do not criticise anyone else's way! I do not know that
there is a best way. There are plenty of good ways. Probably the best way for us would be the one that humbled
us most. If we preened ourselves that nobody else was
following Mass as well as we were, that would be the
worst way for us. There is that difficulty about the modern
liturgical movement. It might become a sort of stunt. The
Liturgy for me is a land flowing with milk and honey; but
I must not despise someone who is saying the Rosary.

That may be far more prayer. For God's sake never let us criticise anybody who is praying. The Pharisee did that, and he was a most loathsome person.

If there is any prayer we ought to say, like going to Holy Mass, let us make that into a personal prayer. The priest's personal prayer is to do what he is told. He has to keep to the rubrics, not to seek personal devotion. The priest is crucified to the least rubric. In some places he is even told where to put his thumb. That is his own personal prayer. God, in His Goodness, has given a kind of spiritual joy in that.

There are, then, the glorious forms of morning and night prayers; bodily prayers; the beautiful traditions of many prayers on your knees. At High Mass you sit a good deal. You do what you are told. Sometimes it would be as well for us to use a kind of bodily prayer for the purpose of humiliation. Individually we may use bodily prayers in some way. It is a tradition in the Church, which I think should be carried out.

Let me go on to speak of the really essential prayer—that is, the Prayer of Petition. By prayer we enter the supernatural order. God has furnished us with all we need in the natural order. We must not pray for the purely natural things God has already given us the power to get for ourselves. In the Lord's Prayer, one petition does seem to be like that—the petition for our daily bread. We have, of course, to use our hands and feet in order to get it. But there is still something that does not depend on us—the crops, the weather. That petition is a magnificent act of faith in God who has providential care of the whole world, and without whose care not even a blade of grass can tremble in the breeze. Of course, we are also praying for the supernatural boon of the Holy Eucharist. But we ask

God, too, that He will fulfil our natural effort by giving us the harvest.

In the supernatural order it is quite different. It would be blasphemy to think that we could reach the supernatural order by ourselves. We cannot lay hold of God by ourselves. We can lose hold of Him. But we can hardly even reach out towards God without His help.

The supernatural must be given. The condition is, it must be asked. Hence the essential prayer of a human being in the presence of the supernatural is to ask. That is why, when the Apostles asked, "Lord, teach us to pray," Our Lord gave instantly that prayer of unparalleled beauty, the "Our Father." It is all petition from beginning to end. We petition for the whole world—for heaven— for our own sinful soul. The essential thing is we must ask God.

If God is prompting us to anything, we shall have an instinctive desire to ask for it. If we ask in His Name something Our Lord would ask for us, God will give that. When we ask for supernatural things in the Name of the Son, that He gives.

The great doctor, St. Thomas Aquinas, teaches us that all our petitions should be for union with God. When we ask for the lesser things, our mistake is not in asking, but in the particular petition which we ask. I often ask people, to make them think, "Meditation isn't prayer, is it? Contemplation isn't prayer, is it?" The devil in a sense is a perfect contemplative. He is always contemplating God —because he hates Him and wants to thwart His purposes. It depends on why you are thinking about God. The Pharisees constantly contemplated Him, in order to ensnare Him. Contemplation itself need not be prayer at all. Love turns contemplation into prayer. People should contemplate because they love God and cannot keep their thoughts away from Him. If you love God, you can hardly help thinking about Him. I remember a dear old lay sister who complained that she did not know how to meditate. I found she was constantly thinking about God the whole of the day. God was in among the dishes. She couldn't keep her eyes off Him. Her union with God went on all day long. She would have been distracted from Him if she had been made to kneel down to pray.

Well, dear children in Jesus Christ, prayer is a most wonderful thing; and I love to think it is easy in many ways. The chief thing is to love God and His Holy and Adorable Will. Then even the supernatural seems to be most natural. Then nothing seems more natural than the supernatural! When we have the heart that loves God and that is weaned from the beauties of this world, it is exceedingly difficult for our soul not to pray and to be united to God.

(The Craft of Prayer)

PERSEVERANCE IN PRAYER

Luke 11:8. Yet if he shall continue knocking, I say to you, although he will not rise and give him, because he is his friend, yet because of his importunity he will rise, and give him as many as he needeth.

Luke 18:1. And He spoke also a parable to them that we ought always to pray and not to faint, saying: . . . Because this widow is troublesome to me, I will avenge her, lest continually coming she weary me.

WHAT is most necessary for us in our spiritual life is some increase in the quality, not in the quantity, of our prayer. Prayer is a central thing in our life. I feel, dear children in Jesus Christ, that Catholics and perhaps the world in general are suffering from a kind of disguised despair. I do not think it is presumption. Presumption is almost too much an act of faith in God. I often think the world's amusements are a sign of despair. It is running away from something. People are clutching at certain things from despair. We must not interpret the modern attitude as just a desire for pleasure. To a large extent it is despair. It is a running away. We have to master these temptations. The soul can easily be stampeded in a crisis. The world is being stampeded now. Even in the spiritual life we have to take a stand and stretch out our arms, as our dear Lord on the Cross. He is on the world's highway, His arms stretched out to prevent our being stampeded.

The first parable is a parable for a man. The other is one for a woman. "Avenge me of mine adversary." The poor widow went on knocking and knocking. The judge said, "She will go on knocking all the night. I had better attend to her."

Both stories are evidence of Our Lord's humour and wisdom. The man says, "A friend has come and I haven't anything in the house." The other man says, "He'll knock until the small hours of the morning. I had better go down." It is a delightful scene. These are delightful stories which our dear Lord told as He was going up to die. Dear Lord, you are very lovely! Let us realise how lovable Our Lord is. When we realise His lovableness, we have gone a long way. This is how He was enlivening the way going up to Jerusalem and death. St. John, I dare say, was in fits of laughter. I love these stories. I love the Story-teller more.

Prayer is some sort of communing with Our Lord.

This is a story of perseverance in prayer. That is the first of the perseverances. We are not very likely to persevere in action unless we persevere in prayer.

When the poor human being begins to drift into the uncertainties of despair, he says, "What is the good of my prayer?" To meet that, our dear Lord tells these two charming stories.

Probably no punishment could be greater than to be given the answer to the prayer we have just made. We do not see that now, but we shall see it in eternity.

So many things prevent us persevering. Perseverance as such is the crown of virtues; and the reward of all virtues. We shall not win the Kingdom of Heaven for charity, but for perseverance in charity; not for patience, but for perseverance in patience; not for humility, but for perseverance in humility. Perseverance is the final perfection of all the virtues.

As soon as we wish to persevere, unforeseeable factors arise. A curious weariness may come in quite suddenly; or distaste—especially if it has been the taste of things rather than their truth which has appealed to us. If the matter of taste is at all predominant in our spiritual life, in twenty-four hours we might have an entire distaste. Tastes come and go. So that perseverance is a very difficult virtue on account of the uncertainty of our spiritual taste. We must avoid enjoying spiritual things that are tasty. There is a sweetness in spiritual things. We say, "Taste and see that the Lord is sweet." But we do not go to them for that. Perseverance is a very difficult duty when it is a question of going to the Faith for some aroma or scent.

Sometimes we are afflicted with weariness benignly by God that we may fasten ourselves on the Rock.

I think we are here dealing with the memory of St. Peter. Our Lord had to say to Peter, "Watch and pray." That means perseverance in prayer, and continuance. It was to Peter especially that the reproach was addressed, "You do not persevere in prayer. Couldst thou not watch?" When Peter failed in prayer, he had simply prepared failure in action. When we fail in prayer we are going to fail in action.

How delightful it is that our Blessed Lord represents Himself as being moved merely by perseverance. It is so beautiful that it is difficult to square it with His Justice, as if He is giving grudgingly what He ought to have given before. "If it was right for me to have it, why didn't You give it at the beginning?" It is as if God says, "One of us will have to give in. Father Vincent, if you don't stop, I suppose I shall have to give in." How lovely art Thou, O Lord! Much lovelier than Thy Tabernacles! There is nothing more human than the Godhead. What we call humanity in ourselves is just a copy of something in Himself. He has the very qualities we call human. Very few of Our Lord's delicious stories are so exquisitely human, humorous and humble as these. I am sure He was making them laugh. It seems topsy-turvy. Usually it is not the man who asks for bread, but the woman. Here it is a man that seeks for bread; and a woman seeking for justice in court! He seems to give the man a woman's parable and a woman the man's! He is trying if by any way He can get them to persevere in prayer.

When people come with a long face and say, "What is the good of praying?" I feel like saying, "Look in the looking-glass! Of course you must persevere. Thank God, we can't get over our faults in a weekend. If we could there is every chance we should be proud. To need more than a weekend gives us at least an opportunity of humility."

When the poor little soul begins to gird at God because He has not answered something, He says, "Go on. Go on." As soon as we start weeding in the garden, the devil sows all the weeds of the British Isles in that particular spot. By pulling some up, we provide another opportunity for them to grow. When you and I try to dig up our faults, it is like loosing the soil; it gives an opportunity for them to sprout out afresh!

Our dear Lord is deeply concerned. "Don't let the poor soul give up its perseverance. It must cheer up. It must almost use its sense of humour, till it grows into a sense of great humility, which is transcendent humour!"

You and I must go on praying. That is why I have not wished to overburden you with extra prayer, but to tell you to add to their quality—to add the delightful quality

of perseverance. Indeed some experienced theologians
and directors will be more concerned by their penitents'
neglect of morning and night prayer than by even grievous bodily sins. They will think that spiritual sins are
more grievous than bodily sins; and that the lack of faith
shown by neglect of prayers is one of the most dangerous
spiritual sins.

Some of our requests God in His mercy has refused.
The soul should go on quite determinedly. It should have
rationed its spiritual life so well that it can go on. Some
people have more zeal and fervour than wisdom. We need
wisdom more than fervour. But we need both the wisdom
and the fervour which make perseverance. We should not
be so much concerned about opening furrows, as of clos-
ing them,—going on to the end. We should be like a
mother nursing her child, going on for months and
months, often feeling tired and pained, but never giving
up. What a lesson, dear children in Jesus Christ! First,
prayer itself; and then, in the spiritual life, too, the lesson
of not giving up those good resolutions which were wise
and of themselves should be eternal and lasting. Things
like prayer are not just for one particular day. They are
for our life here below.

We should pray about the various needs of life. We
must beseech our daily bread. In its essence that means
that we are bound to protect our life. St. Paul said, "If a
man doth not work, neither shall he eat." That was the
little tent-maker who boasted that he was no charge on the
Christian community. What he ate, he earned. We could
say, "Oh, my God, you have put me down in this world.
If I do not have some food and clothing, I shall die. It is
Thy Holy and Divine Will that I should have something
to eat and clothes to wear." When we do what God has

provided us with the power of doing for ourselves, God will in some way help us.

In some special cases there are individuals with terrible diseases. They cannot do a hand's turn. That is God's Holy and Adorable Will. Those people are naturally a little pained in mind. I tell them those who are suffering most are doing most. There is no job in the world like the job of patience on a sickbed. To some God might seem not to be giving daily bread. My heart is wrenched when I think of it. Some are dying with starvation. Probably that is the most difficult temptation to meet. Some poor souls could say, "God doesn't seem to give me even the minimum." But it is a most extraordinary thing (I only see myself one answer), very often those souls that might have a right to say, "Yes, Master, but we ask and do not receive," those who have almost the greatest temptation to say the most cruel things to God—they DON'T. That reproach rarely arises from their lips. From poor starving lips it seldom does. That is their greatness. God help them.

(The Craft of Prayer)

THE PROBLEM OF SUFFERING

Matt. 7:9–11. What man is there among you, of whom if his son shall ask bread, will he reach him a stone? Or if he shall ask him a fish, will he reach him a serpent?

If you then being evil, know how to give good gifts to your children, how much more will your Father who is in heaven give good things to them that ask Him?

ONE of the problems which seems to give the lie to this truth is the great problem of human suffering. It seems to give the lie to the goodness of God.

Much sympathy must always be felt for those who, under pressure of bodily or mental suffering, find that a cloud has come between them and God's goodness.

Now, God is good, and sometimes best when the soul that loves Him is asked to go into the shadows even of death. Well, of course, we never go alone, but always in His company.

Poor human nature, which has almost lost the art of reasoning, thinks that we within the mercies of the Church are morbid about suffering. Of course the contrary is the case. They see we do face it. In a sense, to quote the Greeks at their best, all philosophy is the philosophy of death. There is no chance of right thinking unless we begin to face the facts. Whether there is a God or is not, there is suffering. To deny the good God is to quench the only light of consolation in the Egyptian night of suffering. The bewilderment of mind nowadays is so great, people think the person who will deal with the difficulty is creating it.

I like the great wisdom of the man who came into the fold within the last few years, Mr. G. K. Chesterton, who said: "Some men have their hands clean because they are making the world unclean. Others have their hands unclean because they are making the world clean." The paradox is not the writer's or the artist's, but of fact, expressing it in exact mode. Of course the writer uttered the paradox, but it is the world's paradox. The poor suffering, bewildered world thinks somehow the Catholic Church is causing suffering because it accepts it as a fact, to be accounted for and counteracted. The Church is never allowing suffering merely to reign, but it tries to counteract it. It has not such a Manichaean view of suffering as to say it is an evil so great that no good could be made of it. But it faces the fact as it is.

It is not a final fact, for God is GOOD.

Now let us just examine it quietly and see the Church's attitude towards it.

The Church does not look at suffering as a final thing, nor any kind of evil or defect as a final thing. It would not allow that. God is in His very essence Good, and some evil things He can do nothing but permit, like moral evil. But all other evils, even pain of body, can never be directly willed by God. God can only permit moral evil, to save human free will. Other evils He allows, never for their own sake, but always for some good. God couldn't allow the slightest moan of a child in a moment's pain as an object of desire. If there is any pain we have of any kind, God can no more desire it for its own sake than we can desire that. He can inflict it, but only as, on a child, a teacher or guide inflicts pain as necessary for its good.

Nowadays I think people ought to realise the great aspect of God, because often, in an unintelligent way, they are causing great pain for some ultimate physical good.

So that the modern world might be expected to understand a group that could not regard a sigh or moan as inflicted by God on His beloved children except for some good or other.

The modern world is avoiding the difficulty and thereby creating it. Never in the history of our own people were there so many suicides. The world is flying from suffering and death; seeking to dull, for those that die and to some extent for those that nurse the dying, the approach of death. It is easier to nurse a drugged patient than one that isn't. That comes close upon the heels of murder. Some of us expect to see almost regularised official murder as the world's bewildered answer to the problem of suffering.

Psychologically, too, the proper way of meeting fear is to stand up to it. Fly and it haunts you. That is the psychology of fear. The world is flying from suffering, and increasing it. It is afraid to look on the lineaments of its own kith and kin when dead. That is diminishing human love. Fear is a very poor substitute for love.

God is good. I am putting that first because it is first. If suffering comes upon us and God is blotted out, everything goes with Him.

Our God is Jesus of Calvary. Never think that Calvary came into its own on Good Friday. It is not just a hill of skulls, shrouded in darkness. It is a mountain lit up as a spring morning with the rising sun, bright with youth, clothed with a white garment, honey-sweet, rose-sweet, with forgiving and forgetting love. The loveliest thing in the whole world is the hill where Jesus died.

So that God is good. And if no other thing went with us into the Garden of Agony, at night, and alone, we should be, ah, not alone! God is good and our hand would be in His. We can feel the print of the nails, and, in the stillness, almost hear the breaking of the Sacred Heart, and hear Him say to the bride of the psalm, "*Veni, coronaberis.*"

He is so much, He is ALL. Take Him away and there is no other. Those who take God out of suffering have taken away its only relief. They have left us stark, hopeless, fallen, no Saviour; no Redeemer; no Fellow-sufferer; alone. And alone in a world that, perhaps, in its bitterness, is wishing us out of its care.

But with Jesus, our God, death itself has an answer and suffering a meaning and a purpose, with Him who is never so near as to those who are on His Cross.

What about ourselves? Let us go quietly into the psychology of it.

We shall find that it is sometimes quite easy to do an act of virtue without having that virtue. But the opportunity of acting only from that virtue is when no other motive is present for the doing of the act. If there is a command and no other motive is available for obeying it except the command, then we have to exert the virtue of Obedience. So that in a sense the great opportunity of exercising a virtue is when it costs.

This life is only preparation; a short, brief span before Eternity. Here in this time of preparation we have to form ourselves, and the only opportunity quickly to form ourselves is to accept some suffering. Without opposition (and suffering is the greatest opposition) it is impossible for us, on the whole, to exert our power to its fulness.

A life of pleasure is not necessarily a life of sin, but it is always lower than the heroic. Watch suffering come to the soul that has been striving to grow! It is like growth after a long winter, when spring seems less than a day and summer follows on the heels of winter. The trees seem to leap into life; before almost the buds are out the blossom is there, and before the blossom is off the tree, the fruit is in profusion.

To some souls there is the invitation, and now their life is only God, only God. He is Alpha and Omega, the First and the Last, and straight to Him their heart goes. There are no bypaths. Straighter even than the arrow to its mark goes the soul that has now accepted that invitation. And oh! the peace that comes!

No peace is equal to accepted sorrow. There is a sense of poise, power, stillness, control. Nowhere else is it equalled in the world. Go to the bed of sickness to see what is strong. There is the strength of weakness that smiles at the onslaught of what seems the greatest thing in the world, death. That is strength like the strong woman who could laugh in the day of death. There is perfect poise and power of control.

If, then, you want to see the essence of peace in this world, look into the tear-misted eyes of accepted suffering—suffering, as they say, "sent by God."

I know what I am speaking about. For a Priest, to help him in his last hour, sees these things as no other being sees them. None so blessed as the Priest acquainted with the heroism of accepted suffering. He knows, as even the heroes and heroines themselves do not know, the strength of their apparent weakness, and the peace that means self-control of heart.

So, then, suffering is necessary for heroes and heroines, that souls may be born. Francis Thompson said:

> Nothing begins and nothing ends
> That is not pain and moan,

> We are born in other's pain
> And perish in our own.

As things are, there must be suffering. Very often those who suffer refuse to call it anything but Joy.

Just one last thing. One aspect of our own relationship to suffering is to reassure those that suffer. There are few tests whether we love God. We could only be certain if God Himself gave us the revelation. Almost equal to that revelation, though a little less, is partnership with Jesus Christ in suffering. No other test comes so near to absolute certitude when, so quickly, though with a sense of pain, souls say, in suffering or sorrow, "Thy Will be done."

If a soul loved God, or loved to love God, and would care to know, not that it loves but that it is loved, the great test is partnership with Jesus Christ in the valley of sorrow, or on the hill of death.

One or other of those two partnerships must one day be ours. May God grant us, in the hour of suffering, whatever it may be, the consolation of accepting it and of having thereby the reassurance that we love Him. May we love Him not just in the day, lest it be the day we love rather than Himself; not just in health, lest it be health of limb we love; but when the night of darkness and pain comes to limb or mind, may we think of His wounded limbs and His sufferings, and then, in our love, our suffering will seem but little to accept beside His.

(*The Craft of Suffering*)

Sorrow must enter in. It is not a final thing. But something has happened to human beings, so that now it is an absolute necessity. Some impurities have to be washed away by suffering. But it isn't the final thing.

Sometimes people, even Catholics, are frightened away from the spiritual life. They think it aims at making us miserable. That was a great surprise to me when I got into the religious life at the age of seventeen. I had always been brought up in excellent Catholic circles, priestly circles. But I was immensely surprised and delighted, when I got in, to find that sadness was never considered one of the products of the religious life. Sometimes you had to afflict yourself with bodily austerities—but if you hadn't joy, out you went! Long faces were not considered outward and visible signs of sanctity. If under a penance you sulked—no vocation! you were not sufficient buoyant or joyful.

St. John is at pains to show us that almost the last note of Our Lord was a note of JOY—just when He is going to be put to death.

In our spiritual life, we are going to have mortification, practice in self-control, penance. People think that is a Chamber of Horrors. The Church isn't a Chamber of Horrors. It is a House of Joy—a House of Bread.

Its very joyousness makes it able to support what breaks other people. I have found the greatest and most undisturbed joy in those who suffer most.

With those who do not suffer, if the cat looks the wrong way, they are almost ready to deny the existence of God. Something crosses them, something is not cooked properly—there is a collision with the kitchen, and a week's notice.

No. There must be suffering, sorrow and pain, and loss.

querade as wars of defence, the defence of our own interests when perhaps our interests are indefensible.

Our Lord speaks to Jerusalem of peace, which is the
only achievement. War is sometimes a necessity; it is not
an achievement. No victories are so great as those of
peace. Peace requires heroism and renunciations. Peace
is the great achievement of human society.

St. Thomas teaches that peace is the effect of charity.
Justice will remove the hindrances to peace; but when
you have opened the shutters you have not necessarily
let in the light. I feel that justice now is still to seek—
the necessary justice that is the removal of the obstacles,
the opening of the gates to the love and charity which
alone can bring in peace.

Jerusalem did not know the arts of peace. It knew the
arts of money-making, almost in the Holy of Holies; but
it did not know the arts of peace, the one thing which
would have justified its existence. In a city so many things
must be forgone that we may be in the city. It should
offer great transcendent gifts if one is to give up these
Surrey downs or the Spring breeze, or the patch of green
moss I saw today on the Common. That was a thing God
had made, and, of course, made for me. A gipsy-man up
there asked me, did I want a carpet? they were difficult
to sell and times were hard. I didn't want a carpet. I went
along the Common. God, the Carpet-weaver, had made a
lovely green carpet, all for me. God made that green
moss for me. I shall have to give that up when I return
to N.W.5. Only God's command to me would bring me
back. Then I will go. This I will give up for Him.

St. Thomas Aquinas says we can have peace with
others only if we have peace in our own soul. Ah, wizard
Doctor, how intricate, as a perfect web, is your thought!

Love sets the ultimate order in all things. Love alone can give peace. Peace has its victories first at home, the peace of love, not of the sword. Only when we are at peace within ourselves is there possibility of that love extending so that we are at peace elsewhere.

"If thou also hadst known the things that are to thy peace!" I didn't know. Oh, the evil of ignorance that comes from some stubbornness or flaw in the human will. "I did not know the things that were to my peace." Is there any phrase that seems to recur so much to our mind when we feel contrite before Our Lord?

"My Master, Thou art weeping—weeping because I do not weep. My well of tears is still dry, until Thou dost water it with Thy tears. Thou art teaching my soul to weep, to know the things that are to my peace."

Tears are mightier than the sword. When tears come, the adversary is often overcome. It argues much for the hardness of that city that it could hear, as it were, the drip of Our Lord's tears and remain the same.

Well, dearest children in Jesus Christ, we must consider Our Lord weeping. That should be one of the scenes we love to contemplate. Even if it is with a kind of stoniness of heart that we watch those tears while we are dry-eyed, yet we may prize them and be very glad that St. Luke, the beloved physician, has dared to recall them. Perhaps St. Peter hardly dared to speak of Our Lord's weeping; he couldn't bear to have the same page speak of his own sin-begotten tears and the Tears of Christ. I can see him in the Catacombs, talking to a small group, like you. If he had spoken of the tears of Jesus there might have been a terrible scene. His own tears would fall in a torrent. Perhaps he had tried and tried again, but had had to go on and speak of something else. "The things which are to thy peace." St. Peter would say: "Oh, I remember that! How little did I know it was meant as much for me as for Jerusalem. I didn't know. My Master's tears must have been flowing for me. Yet so delicately did He chide me that I did not know He was chiding me. I thought Him almost unmanly, that He was showing a certain weakness, incompatible with a great leader. Now I know. He was weeping for me."

I have only dared to touch this theme of the tears of Christ as a scientific or statistical account. Those tears seem to open up the mystery of the Sacred Heart almost more than the Crucifixion.

It is terrible that He could have wept just to think of the state of something He loved. Oh, how wonderful is the Sacred Heart of Our Lord!

St. Peter says so beautifully, we are redeemed not with gold or silver, but with the Precious Blood, the dear Blood, of Christ. We are bought with His Blood. Now we see that we are bought also with His tears. You can, in spite of a man, make his heart's blood flow; you cannot make him weep. You can shed his blood; you cannot shed his tears. This is the Priest and Victim offering Himself. They are tears from His very heart of heart. And we are bought at that great price. We know how much we should be to ourselves. We know the things that should be to our peace, because we know the things that set Him weeping.

How soon our tears would be dried if we knew the things that are to our peace? If there is anything in us that makes us not in peace, may His tears give us the power of a flood of tears to wash those things away.

"Oh, my Beloved Master, let me see the things that are to my peace. If there is anything between me and Thy

Holy Will, let me take that from my life, or take my life from me.

Once, in the hour of Thy greatest anguish, Thou didst speak of peace, and didst promise that it would abide in me.

Thou has come into my bereft soul to give it peace. Give me grace to weep with Thee, tears from my heart that can hardly bear to think of Thy sufferings without itself suffering death and crucifixion.

(The Craft of Suffering)

THE MERCY OF GOD

John 11:3. His sisters therefore sent to him, saying: Lord, behold, he whom thou lovest is sick.

I HAVE READ this passage out because it is part of the Holy Gospel for the day. You may have noticed that we stood up longer than usual. This is another proof that daily Mass is a great banquet. The Body and Blood of Our Lord is not only food, but food for thought. The Word became Flesh that we might have something to think about—something worth thinking about. Everybody in this great world of ours is thinking about something. Some thoughts are such that it would be more profitable to think of nothing! Some thoughts are a sort of living death. But daily Mass supplies us with something to think about. As years go on, God has allowed me to see more clearly that the thing set before us in Holy Mass is the best approach for all the other things we shall have to think about during the day. I feel a sort of qualm of conscience if I don't found any retreat I am giving on the Gospel which Holy Mother Church sets before us at the spread table of Holy Mass.

I feel as if Mother Church says to me, "Now, Father Vincent, that is what I put before my children today. Will you kindly take my children out for a walk and tell them about it?" I feel like a nursery-maid commissioned by the mother to take the children out into the fresh air for a certain length of time. I want to be very faithful to those instructions and that guidance, otherwise I don't know what would happen to the poor little freight in the perambulator!

Once one sets one's eyes on the beautiful things of the Gospels, it is almost impossible to think of anything else. It is like having the sun in our eyes. We can see nothing except the sun. Other things that once seemed beautiful now seem almost dull and commonplace.

This is such an academy of beauty, I hardly know where to begin.

Here is a unique study in the relationship of Jesus to individual souls, in a little home. In the Gospels we have the relationship of Jesus to Peter; the less detailed relationship to John; there are many instantaneous sketches of His relationship to souls. Many disappear. I often wonder what the widow of Naim did for Jesus afterwards. Did she always love Him? They are swiftly moving pictures; like the daughter of Jairus and the whole household of Jairus. Jesus goes into it for an instant and then disappears.

But in this story we have an account of very detailed relationship to individual souls. If this is Mary Magdalen, the sinner, look at the very detailed study of the Incarnate Word to a little home. If she really was the Sinner, the tragedy of the home becomes very deep.

Those who have had many brothers and elder sisters know the extraordinary love that can exist between them. In English literature there is the example of Charles Lamb and his sister, an exquisite incident in English literature, like an unwritten poem.

Here we have a home; two sisters, one of whom perhaps was the source of very great sorrow to a brother and another sister. Our Lord loved them. St. Luke has given us another study of Martha and Mary; Martha busy through her great love of Jesus; Mary with her own game of sitting still and allowing the Word of God to be the Counsel for her defence.

Blessed are we when God takes up the Counsel for our defence!

Perhaps a sister generally loves a brother more than he loves her. Here is the awful study of what comes upon the little group by the sickness and death of one who was their pride.

It is again something for us to think about.

They sent off to Jesus. They made Him at once acquainted with his sickness. Death often follows quickly in those parts, like a sirocco, a typhoon. Jesus was so much part of that family that they sent Him at once news of his sickness. "Behold, he whom Thou lovest is sick." That is a phrase that has entered into the vocabulary of mysticism.

Though God never loves sin, yet He loves the sinner—not for his sin, not for the one rift that has now come into the creature of His fashioning. But God loves His creatures. We are the offspring of God, and even, in a sense, our sickness of soul makes God's love, as it were, hotter. The mother that has a sick child doesn't love it more than when it is well, but she is now offering more services of love. Love is a giving. She gives more. Not more love, but more services and signs of love.

When we are sick to death, in sin, God's love seems to be fanned to white heat, and He gives us services that at other times of health are not needed. He does not love the lost lamb more than the ninety-nine, but He seems to love it more, it needs more. They that need less are not loved less. Equal love of souls, in unequal stress, demands unequal services. Here is that most touching phrase, uttering emotion we can never utter. When we are before God, with an overwhelming sense of our own weakness, we feel like a poor strayed lamb, which had gone into the marshland and hardly knows which way to turn, faintly bleating that someone may hear. In our bleating, what we say is this: "He whom Thou lovest is sick. He whom Thou lovest is strayed. I have lost Thee. I cannot find Thee. Find me. Seek me. I cannot find Thee. I have lost my way. Thou art the Way. Find me, or I am utterly lost. Thou lovest me. I do not know if I love Thee; but I know Thou lovest me. I do not plead my love, but Thine. I do not plead my strength, but Thine. I do not plead my deed, but Thine. He whom Thou lovest is sick.

"I dare not say: 'He who loves Thee is sick.' My sickness is that I do not love Thee. That is the source of my sickness which is approaching death. I am sinking. Raise me. Come to me upon the waters. He whom Thou lovest is sick."

That would be a perfect phrase when you and I are preparing to come in our sin and ask God to show us those sins; to show our poor sin-blinded heart its sin. We may be so accustomed to our sins, the lesser ones, that we are blinded to them. Or we hug them and think they are needed, as the sick think the bed they lie on the safest and happiest place in the world.

Instantly, of course, our blessed Lord says: "Let us go." In the previous chapter of St. John's Gospel, the tenth—the beautiful chapter of the Good Shepherd—the Jews had made that most terrible and tragic attempt to stone Our Lord. And yet, of course, the love that brought Him down to earth was not finally to be conquered by the threat of death. It is a sign of His great love that for ONE—ONE—not for the whole people, not for the whole

world—but for ONE whom He loves—Lazarus—He went
back. He had been safeguarded hitherto. A vision sent
Him to Egypt when danger threatened; from the moment
of the Incarnation a thousand angels were between Him
and hurt. But now, not for a soul's sake, but just for love's
sake, He went back into the heart of danger.

Had St. John not written this, we should never have
known this account of friendship and perfect love.

Of course, in a sense, it was a choice between stonings.
A love that shirks the service of love is subject to pitiless
stoning. Jesus never hesitated. He had set His mind to
go back to the human heart visited by sorrow.

Well, dear children in Jesus Christ, if, as St. Thomas
says, all meditation should end in our greater realisation of
God's Mercy and our own misery, from our depths of
misery we may cry out to His still greater Mercy. That
Mercy is here; Mercy, and the most sweet love of Jesus:
the music of God's Infinite Love.

"Lazarus, our friend, sleepeth." Even death, to the
touch and love of Him who created life, is only Sleep.
From the very depths of the tomb and the corruption
of the tomb God can bring life, as if death had been only
sleep. There is no utter death for Him who created life.

"Lazarus is dead." You can build on death as you can
build on life. On those great facts you can make a unity
and a base. Whilst life is trembling in the balance for
days or months, nothing definite can be done. But once
life has left the body—if the father is dead, or the mother
is dead, the support of the household is dead—you can
begin to build. You build another life for yourself; that
is the one undeniable immovable basis of whatever else
is to be.

Into this house of sorrow there came the Incarnate

Word—from some distance—into the zone of danger—and exchanged and took the place of Lazarus. For whereas today Lazarus was dead and Jesus alive, before the week is out, Lazarus is alive and Jesus is dead. There was much love given to Lazarus, greater than Jonathan gave David—given to sinful man, and given to you and me. We can build on life and build on death. One thing is stronger—the love of Jesus.

I know not what else in my life can be accepted as lasting—my fitful efforts towards good? my lapses into sin? Something outside myself is lasting, the everlasting love of Him who made me and bore with me. His love towards me is greater than the love I bear myself. On that alone, on the love of my Redeemer, can I build. On that everything in my soul has to be built.

O, my Master, I will build my soul anew in Thee. Only let Thy love come into it and make it Thy dwelling place, a temple worthy of Thee.

(*God's Way of Mercy*)

GOOD TIDINGS

Matt. 28:2. And behold there was a great earthquake. For
an Angel of the Lord descended from Heaven and, coming, rolled back the stone and sat upon it.

I HEARD LATELY, dear children in Jesus Christ, that at a
recent conference on psychology one of the accredited
teachers of psychology—I don't know if he had any particular creed—made the remark that gradually he had
found the great book on psychology was the Bible. And,
dear children in Jesus Christ, in this wonderful scene
there are marvels of psychology, marvels of the action of
the human mind and the human will under great doings.

We have here a wonderful scene, described so perfectly in a few words of the inspired writer that any
other words, even of the greatest master of words—and
of course any words of mine—must be an insult.

All I should ever attempt to do would be to call your
attention to the story; as if, suddenly turning round, I
had seen the sun rising with great beauty, and I asked you
to turn and look at it; to turn your eyes from the remnants
of the night in the West, eastward to the beauty of the
dawn. I can only ask you to turn the eyes of your soul;
ask you to put yourselves in the place of these women;
to be for the moment Mary Magdalen. We must all be
that great Saint and play her part, her glorious part of
sorrow and love.

We must go up with her. There are two of us, like the

two Marys, going up with perhaps fear in our heart, and yet a love that conquers fear.

To go out to a tomb in the dark—the tomb of one lately laid there—must have had its terrors. And yet there was some life of love in their hearts that laid their fears to rest—that put their fears almost to death. We can wonder what these women were expecting; what they expected to see and to do. Many would have thought they were going on a fool's errand; a newly made tomb and a great stone. No woman's hand, even strengthened by love, could move it. Of course, love undertakes and often achieves impossibilities, if it is only pressed forward by Divine Love. If the hand is only impelled by the omnipotence of God, no stone, even the greatest, can bar the way that reaches to the Beloved.

There is the account in St. Matthew's Gospel of that splendid coming of an Angel, and the glorious royal salvoes, as it were, which the earth gives; not just quaking with fear, but, in the splendid metaphor of the old Psalmist, like water "clapping its hands with joy." The earth which has entombed so many dead rejoices that it now has the power of bringing forth the living from its dead womb; and, for very joy, as it were, it claps its hands.

The stone is rolled back. I love to think of that stone being rolled back. And I love to ask God to lay His Hand on the so many stones that need rolling back in my own soul, that He may enter in. He is standing so patiently at the door and knocking. May He roll away those stones that are so great it is almost impossible to hear Him knocking.

I love to think of the rolling stone. "O, my Divine Master, lay Thy Hand, Thy nail-pierced Hand, on this stone in my soul. Roll it away; crush it to the very dust, that the gates of my soul may be lifted up and Thou, my King, mayest come and be enthroned where so many others have sat as sovereign for a while, giving me no joy."

How gracious it was of God to send an Angel. The Angel always seems to me like a sister of Our Lady and St. Mary Magdalen rather than a brother of St. Peter; so chaste, so pure, so virgin-like. No wonder one of those unsullied courtiers of God was sent so courteously to give these women tidings of great joy.

Of course, I presume there were armies of them unseen, unheard in the sky. When He came at midnight the armies were seen, as the great winter lights against the darkness of the night. But only two were seen this morning; and He Himself will just appear in all the shining beauty of His new life.

Words sent from Heaven are always sent for us; and we can think again and again of the words He said through His Angel, to these God-sent women, who, one would have thought, could hardly move from shock. The soldiers were as dead men. But these women were now alert with the strength of God!

Such is the power of grace that the weak, strengthened by God, may stand and walk. And if we ever see our own weakness, after ten thousand falls and forgivings, and do not see what the strength of God can do through our weakness, then we have almost forgotten God, and the God we worship is not omnipotent. What can omnipotence not do with you and me?

What words the Angel says! "Fear not you." Words from Heaven are always creative words. They effect what they signify; they do what they say. They are no sooner said than done. If God says: "Fear not," then fear is either quelled or prevented.

"Fear not you, for I know that you seek Jesus who was crucified." Those words would make an entire retreat. "I know that you seek Jesus Crucified." Every word is a profound mystery. There are no other words like these, not even in St. Thomas Aquinas. "Fear not you, for I know that you seek Jesus Crucified." The profound psychology of that! the knowledge of the human soul! Fear, as you know, is never either a first or a last emotion of the soul. The first and last must be Love. There is a fear that must be cast out, or it will cast out all of value in our soul. But that fear will be cast out if we seek Jesus Crucified. And that is what, as it were, by our Baptism we do profess. Some day you will assist at a Baptism. You will find it one of the most valuable meditations you could possibly make, especially if you assist at a Baptism of an adult—if the priest carries out the glorious ceremonies of the Baptism of an adult. The other day I had the great privilege of administering the Sacrament of Baptism to an unbaptised man almost in mid-life. You should try to assist at one and count the number of times the Sign of the Cross is made and see where it is made. All the senses of the body are signed with the Holy Cross. If I could have a grievance—it would only be a psychological grievance—against authority it would be that the glorious ceremonies of Adult Baptism are almost unknown. I know no meditation so glorious. The Priest signs the whole body with the Cross of Jesus Crucified. The whole body is anointed for suffering—not that we are going to create suffering; we are going to meet it, to overcome it.

Suffering comes to all alike. All alike do not meet it. All do not know its message to them, the treasure that is there, hidden under the garment of suffering.

And so, when we seek Jesus of Nazareth, Jesus Crucified—as the Beloved must always seek the Beloved— there is nothing to fear, except the Divine thing. All other fears are put out of the room—as Jesus put the wailers out of the room.

(But, dear children, we must get on! These things are so full of thought, it is almost impossible to tear oneself away!)

Oh, my dear Jesus, if Thou wert saying this to me now! "I know that you seek Jesus." What consolation and peace that would bring!

But the Divine message seems often so homely, so simple—as simple as our dear Lord's raising the little one from death to life and saying so simply, "Give the little one something to eat," and in the hurry and preparation probably He steals away. That is a little trick of His! That goes to your heart almost more than the miracle! Now you see the same thing.

These words are almost throbbing with new job. "He is Risen!" "Come and see." That little phrase is used once or twice in the Gospels—once when John and Andrew said so shyly, "Where do You live?" Our dear Lord smiled and said: "Come and see." The angel, as it were, is saying the same thing. "Come and see." "And going quickly." Now we have the first great indication of quick movement, that Easter hurry and haste. I was thrilled the other day, when one of the Maltese Fathers told me that in Malta on Easter Day they have a glorious procession; it starts about three in the morning and lasts till nine-thirty; and part of the procession is carrying a great

statue of Our Lord Risen, very heavy indeed. In one part
they run up a hill. I think there is no mention of the group
round Our Lord running.

"Quickly," says the Angel. Our Lord had said to Judas,
"What thou dost, do quickly."

Now, the good news is GOOD. It must be taken quickly
to the whole world. The little thing called Jewry has
now a message to the world: "This is the day." They have
to carry to the whole world the message of Jesus Christ's
life from death, with forgiveness for the sins of the world.

"Go quickly." It is almost to the credit of those women
that they ran; they went down hill quickly, running, a
dangerous thing to do—to tell the good news. Alas, you
know, sometimes bad news travels fastest. We should
never give wings to bad news!

I will just refer to the great thought in the mind of
the Holy Father at the present time, and in the mind of
all those looking at the world through the mind of Christ.
Bad news that thinks itself good news is spreading like
wildfire. We have invented such extraordinary things that
a war of a few years destroys millions more than wars of
centuries. We have invented such marvels that a lie can
get at the ears of the world within an hour. Quicker than
the feet of these women sped by an angel, comes terrible
news today; and those who seek their pleasures in that
way will hear very few Gospels, very few. But they may
hear the Master of Lies quoting Scripture (as he did!),
and offering something to their understanding.

Well now, we hear the words "Catholic Action." These
women were not told to remain on the hill of contemplation, but to go very quickly, as if they had just lost a little
time. "Tell them you have something worth carrying,

worth hearing. Go out into the world and tell the good news." Good news ought to have winged feet; it often has feet of lead; it often has feet and ears of lead.

This is a very practical thing for us; because our spiritual life can never be self-rounded.

It would be worthwhile, each one of you, just taking count next week how many you meet who are not Catholics and have not any idea of the thing you are listening to. But oh! dear children in Jesus Christ, an old priest like myself seems to realise more and more, we mustn't go out into the world as if the world were our enemy and we have to conquer it. It is like the poor wounded man on the road to Jericho; it is hungry, and we want to give it something to eat; thirsty and we want to give it something to drink; homeless, and we want to open the door and give it a lodging and a home. It is not an enemy we want to overcome and subdue. We have some glorious thing, some Light, we want those outside to share; like the sunshine. We want it to be theirs as much as ours. And I think the first argument, and probably the most effective, is our life. But it is no use our speaking of our life if our life doesn't speak for itself! The first apologetic, and possibly the best, is our life, but it must be a life that speaks for itself. We can speak of God's Mercy to us, of His Mercy shown to sinners of whom I am chief. Ah! then we can speak of ourselves, and tell them of the extraordinary Mercy of God in taking pity on such sinners as we are. We must somehow or other fulfil our duty of spreading the good news. Can you imagine anything so out of touch with the emotions of Mary Magdalen and the other Mary as having to go and tell the other people? It seems almost a heartless message. But God didn't come into the world just for Mary Magdalen. She would not have known the reward which, within an hour, was to be hers —that she would be the first to see the Risen Body and hear Him for the first time call her by her name.

We may fitly close our Recollection with the exquisite scene from the pen of St. Mark—really from the lips of Peter. "But He, rising early the first day of the week, appeared first to Mary Magdalen, out of whom He had cast seven devils." [1]

What we look on as good news, others look on as bad tidings—so bad they have hardly anything bad enough to say even of the messengers. It is quite common to be called a liar. But the message is not a lie. And here is an exquisite story of how, first of all, that great woman, St. Mary Magdalen, was commissioned to go and broach the good tidings of the Resurrection.

"The first day of the week"—that day, of course, began not just a new week but a new era. The old rocks were the same as ever and the sun the same sun that had gone down in sorrow on Good Friday. But it was really a new world. And it is of extraordinary interest, and something very deliberate and designed, that the first appearance of our blessed Lord was to no other than to the official sinner. The first external manifestation of the Risen Christ and of His Love was to that official sinner "out of whom He had cast seven devils."

She goes off to announce to the world not just the fact that Jesus has risen, but that everything else has risen. I suppose the world should be in tears. It is in tatters anyhow. Worse than eyes that have too many tears are those that have none. Mary Magdalen goes off and finds those who are expected to do things weeping and mourn-

[1] Mark 16:9.

ing. She tells them the good news, and they do not believe.

When you offer to those that suffer the only consolation you have to offer, they seem to refuse it. God's doings are so good, they seem to astound us by their gener-
osity. He is most bounteous. The niggardliness is on our
side. When you come to my term of years—a long stretch
to look over and very little to look forward to except
eternity—you see days when you were inclined to think
God hard and not understanding—almost cruel. Now the
mere passing of the years brings vision, and in all that is
seen we see not just the hand of God, but the Love of
God.

If there is any weeping, it is for our past weakness, not
for anything God has done. Nothing He has given brings
forth our tears, but all we have withheld, all we have
misunderstood. How terrible it is when the soul is in anger
with God—like a poor befevered child that struggles in
its mother's arms when she wishes to solace it. Human
nature still plays so foolish a game as not believing the
good tidings when they are told, and not accepting king-
doms when they are offered.

It is impossible to disappoint God; and so the greet-
ing that met Mary Magdalen's news did not disappoint
Him. St. Luke develops the story by telling of those two
fugitives whom Jesus joined, and brought back to the
city in peace. The poor human heart is so suspicious of
God, it almost again refused to believe; and again Jesus
was not disappointed. From our human point of view,
His conduct might almost be called folly. It seems impossible to insult God. When people seem almost dull,
you say, "You know, you couldn't insult them!" It means
a certain dullness. We can't insult the dog that barks at

us. We say we can't insult certain people—as in utter condemnation. We seem unable to insult them.

We cannot really disappoint God. He has pity for us, He knows the heart of our desires and often sees in words that are of hate a kind of incipient babbling of love.

And so now Jesus rises; and rises, of course, with the thing for which He came into the world—forgiveness, perfect forgiveness.

I don't think I know my Jesus until I know Him as Jesus, my Redeemer. There is such joy, when we have ill-treated others, in the thought of their forgiveness, that we can almost sing—*"Felix culpa."* It is almost worth while to have sinned. Jesus forgives so perfectly. He has only chidden us because we didn't believe. We thought His love could fail. We did not trust Him or love Him enough. We can only fall at the feet of the world which rejects Him—go down on our knees, as He went down— and offer them the love which is first and best in human life, that they may enter into the love which is first and best in Eternal Life.

I think when we consider this beautiful scene, we should not only think of our own sins, but how those imperfections of ours have stood in the way of our being Apostles and speaking the message every one of us has to speak. You have a way of approach the Priest has not. And it must be the announcing of the Good News so set in a casing of Joy that others will be called to it by the very joy it seems to give the teller.

I am quite sure our message to the world must be somehow or other the remembrance of Easter Joy, like Merrie England, something mirthful and lightsome and joyous, that will at once make us more conscious of our sin and more glad that our Redeemer liveth.

God grant us to have the assurance and then the obedience and swiftness of foot of these women, who came running down even to the Apostles with the message of the Risen Christ.

(*God's Way of Mercy*)

CONFESSION

Mark 2:5. Son, thy sins are forgiven thee.

THIS IS ONE of the most striking scenes in the Gospel, evidently of very great importance because recorded by Matthew, Mark and Luke—common to the Synoptists, as we say.

We have here a unique story. I should just like to speak to you of sin and its forgiveness. Sin is an old word, now consecrated by the official use of the Church of God.

I feel more and more the necessity of speaking in old words. That is what we do in all the other sciences. We do not change the old words. Grass is still grass. Roses are still roses. If the science grows, or discovers some new thing, it gives the new thing a new name. But the old words remain. Electricity is still electricity; wind is still wind; the sun is still the sun. Though a very great deal has been found out about the sun, it is still called sun. Astronomy has kept the old words. It has added thousands and thousands of planets to our knowledge. It has increased not the firmament, but our knowledge of the firmament. The old words remain. Things would be topsy-turvy if what today we call the sun tomorrow we called the moon.

It is very remarkable that, in affairs of the mind, especially of the soul, people often don't like the old words. It seems as if the one unpardonable sin now is to use an old word. New words are invented for the old things.

This is peculiar to the mental sciences—fatal in affairs of the soul!

I often quote my own great teacher, St. Thomas Aquinas, who has not added one word. I have spent over forty years with him and have not discovered one word he has invented. Nowadays some people make several words with their first book.

Old words, such as S-I-N, show profound philosophy, profound depths.

Here we have a scene full of old words; a string of wonderful words. I do counsel you to take a word and let it remain in your mind.

We have read the account from St. Mark's Gospel—and therefore St. Peter's preaching. Perhaps he preached this to a group of Roman matrons, gathered in one of the private houses, or it might have been in a catacomb. He is qualified to describe the scene. It took place in his house, a fairly large one in Capharnaum, somewhere down by the brink of the Lake; there would be St. Peter's house, with its flat roof. It is very remarkable; I need not do more than suggest to you that the first great sermon on the forgiveness of sin was preached in the house of St. Peter. There our blessed Lord chose to dwell as a lodger. When the official came to collect the tax, our blessed Lord was technically and legally a lodger in that house. To a large extent He is still a lodger in the house of Peter.

It is a strange fact, a man was brought with a bodily ailment and, in the most inconsequent (almost rude!) way, our blessed Lord said: "Son, *thy sins be forgiven thee.*"

That had never been heard in the world before; it was a unique thing. If you read through the books of the Old

Testament, you will notice that sometimes they put before you the idea of Sin. The Jews had quite a clear idea of offending Jehovah; that singled them out from the other nations. David, in his psalm, says: "To Thee only have I sinned." They had the idea, too, of external offences being taken away by external confession. The whole idea of Sacrifice centres round the idea of external offerings through an official, the priest. Every organisation must have some official to act for the others. The Jews had the idea of public faults against the Law being taken away by the official priesthood. What we do not find really, in the Old Testament, is the idea of the taking away of internal guilt. It is difficult to believe they realised it. We often look back on the Old Testament with the eyes of the New Testament. But the coming of Jesus Christ into the world has deepened the meaning of words. I spoke of St. Thomas Aquinas; but it is a remarkable thing that our blessed Lord, the *Word*, never added a new word. He spoke a language that had one of the smallest vocabularies. Very few words did our blessed Lord use. The greatness of His Word is that it expressed much in little. Do not be surprised, therefore, if our blessed Lord uses the same old words but deepens their meaning. The wells are dug still deeper. The word sin is completed as the sense of sin against Good deepens. Jesus Christ has come into the world to forgive sin. That is quite new. In some way, it is another mode of forgiving. Sin will be taken away. There was a customary phrase, "saving us from sin," but now the meaning of it is deepened. The mercies of God are being increased.

With the idea of God's forgiveness comes a deeper idea of the guilt of sin. The very guilt of sin is deepened. We see its effects. It does not merely require repentance. It also needs forgiveness—external and official pronouncement of its forgiveness. It is not sufficient for us to repent. God must forgive.

Here we have a most perfect study of the whole idea of that great institution of Christ our Lord Himself, the Sacrament of Penance, or Confession—the statutory or legal forgiveness of sin. Almost every word has something to do with that. "Brought"; a complete sinner cannot go back himself to God; he has to be brought by someone else. That is so much a matter of conviction in my own mind that I constantly ask, as a mere matter of delight: "Who has been praying for you? What has happened to you to give you the extraordinary grace of repentance? Who has brought you? Who were the four who brought you?" It is a recurrent phenomenon in the great grace of coming into the Catholic Church. Hardly anyone receives that grace without having been borne to Jesus Christ by the prayers of others. Sometimes they don't know. Later on they may know. One hasn't the faintest idea how many owe the gift of their own repentance to the prayers of others. That makes us humble.

Our blessed Lord knows what is in the heart. He is omniscient. He knows what is in the heart before the heart has spoken. You cannot deceive the one who reads your heart. All that is in this wonderful study.

We have a profound study of the dispositions of this man. He is afflicted with a bodily ailment. It may have been temporal punishment to a large extent. How efficacious a sermon is some bodily punishment. Some souls are not brought to the sense of their spiritual ailments until they have a bodily affliction or temporal affliction. That is the whole philosophy of temporal punishment. It is also instructive. It opens the eyes to the possibility of spiritual punishment for spiritual disease. If persons won't open their eyes to spiritual ailments by temporal ailments, there is no other means. It is the last resource, not the first, nor the highest. It is not the most perfect soul that is drawn to think of God by bodily ailments. It is the last hope. If not that, death.

A great deal of human unhappiness is entirely due to the human will—not necessarily in the person who is unhappy. But banish human sin for a week, and a great number of ailments would disappear. Specialists in sin are the great modern need. We will never cure on a large scale without constantly teaching of sin. There are some of us who feel at the present time that our country is heading for bankruptcy. I imagine the great cause of that would be sin. Numbers of free wills are doing wrong; I do not say any particular class, but if sinners constitute a class, then it is a class. The effects are inevitable—unless we try to avoid them, by avoiding committing sin.

Well now, dear children in Jesus Christ, the Church—that is, Jesus Christ—has instituted the external tribunal of mercy, giving grace, on the condition of human repentance. That external tribunal in a sense need never be used, because we are bound only to confess mortal sin. The forgiveness of sin, as it existed before Jesus Christ came into the world, is entirely untouched—sins forgiven by turning to God and calling on His mercy. Most people have their sins forgiven before they come to Confession. There is not the faintest obligation to confess venial sin. If our life were led absolutely without mortal sin, we should not be obliged to go to Confession. The statutory rule is that once a year you are expected to present yourself.

But if we have sinned grievously, we are obliged to

present ourselves to the officials of the Church of Christ. Why? What is the beautiful philosophy behind that? No sin, especially no great sin, is just a harm done to the individual who commits it. I believe myself that the future of the human race is bound up with that idea. The soul that is conscious of a grievous sin is conscious of a great harm done to the community—to someone else. That common hurt should now be forgiven. What a profound thought that is!—almost the most unselfish thought about sin.

There is a kind of heroic sinner who is not influenced by the effect of sin on himself, but is deeply stirred at the thought of hurting someone else. You cannot frighten such as him by telling them of the effect—even the eternal effect—on themselves. It is very difficult in time to realise eternity. To them Hell is not a threat, it is just a rude word. It seems to fasten them in their sin. But let them realise they are hurting someone they love—that moves them. If they are such persons that they don't love anybody, I don't know what is to be done!

That is one of the most profound ideas about this divine institution of the Sacrament of Penance. It is an institution manifestly divine. No human thought could have instituted it. Nobody is as addicted to Confession as I am. I have been dogging it since my seventh year—every week; sometimes several times a week, my soul tortured by its sin. I always speak with thankfulness of having received those great mercies. I often feel more grateful to God for Confession than for Holy Communion. The sense of relief and peace is more intense. That is why I speak of it—poor miserable sinner who has dogged God in His Mercies in that way.

I have felt of late that Confession of our sins to the

Church is a Divine institution to bring to our mind that we belong to the Church.

We cannot go alone to God. We belong to His Mystical Body, the Church; by even our most secret sins, if they be grievous, we have injured the Mystical Body of Jesus Christ and must ask forgiveness of His Mystical Body, too. That is sound theology. Some people think the more we can eliminate the Church the better. That is all wrong. We are borne to Christ our Lord by others.

In the incident of the man sick of the palsy, our blessed Lord says three things:

Arise;
Take up thy bed.
Go into thy house.

They are three, and in the right order. You and I can think about them.

Confession is something which helps us to arise. We hear of Progress. Progress is going on and on and on, but not necessarily going up. It might be going down. The Church says: "Come up"—a much better word. "Come up higher." That is God's invitation. Whenever a soul wishes to get out of the mire of sin, it goes to Confession. The priest has only one medicine. It is the right medicine. Is it the priest's medicine? He didn't make it. God made it. We have only one medicine, God's; out of God's pharmacopoeia. Confession. Begin there—to be forgiven if we are in deep sin—or if we want to go higher; if we have been kept out of sin by the grace of God and we feel we would like to be more closely related to God. Our soul may not be in grievous sin. God alone has the secret. But that is the right way to begin. There is God's medicine.

When I first mentioned to a priest that I wanted to

become a religious (I said to myself, I don't want to go
to Hell; I think I will go to the noviciate. I made the
choice between the noviciate and Hell. That is the way
I put it at seventeen years of age. It was entirely un-
sentimental. Hell was a geographical expression to me),
I went to Confession, to my old confessor. He said: "You
think about it for some time; think about it for three
months; then make up your mind; and then act." That
is wisdom. Isn't that wise? I wanted to try to keep out of
Hell. I went into the confessional. Oh, the extraordinary
laboratory wisdom of it!

It is so simple, like two and two make four.

> Think over it;
> Make up your mind;
> Act.

Here I am, speaking about the wisdom given to me in
my seventeenth year, exactly as if our blessed Lord had
invented the Sacrament of Confession for Father Vincent
McNabb when discussing what to do with his wretched
little soul.

And so I arose—much against my will in many ways.

The next thing is to walk. We must be self-possessed.
Our feet have to be our own. After illness our feet are
not our own. We can't walk. But in the spiritual life there
is no convalescence. God has found our feet for us. Our
feet are now our own. We own ourselves. We have been
bought at a great price, and then given back to ourselves.
"Father Vincent, you have lost yourself. Here you are!
I make you a present of yourself!" "Really! I am myself!
I own myself! I own my own will. I can put one foot
before the other. I can go up." It is very difficult to go
up. That is why we have lifts.

Now our feet are our own. We own ourselves. How

wonderful that is! The soul that has used God's institution of mercy, in Confession, now gets the ownership and possession of his own soul. Sometimes when I am beset in a public park by the word "Progress," I just stampede that objection by saying: "One hundred years ago everyone had a house. Hands up all of you who have a house." I asked that, last Sunday in Hyde Park; only one hand went up. It was a Jewish hand! And he said: "I am going to sell it!"

By sin we give up possession even of our own soul. We have hardly even the leasehold. We are lodgers. It is not our own. It is more or less a furnished flat where sin has gained possession. When that sin has been taken away by God's forgiveness, we are once more owners of our own soul. It becomes our own; the house will be ours—God's dwelling, and that means HOME. "Home means someone somewhere." Home means love somewhere; and, where God is dwelling, Love is in the heart. Our heart becomes our home, and we are at home with ourselves.

Imagine the homelessness of a human being not at home with himself! A homeless wanderer in this great world.

The human heart that has received God's Mercies in Confession becomes full of Grace. Perhaps souls do not realise that the scientific use of Confession will furnish the soul and give it the possibility of challenging everything.

I love the quaint story of the Michael Fields—those two great women poets whom it was my privilege to know. They had a very beautiful and most artistic house at Richmond. They spoke to a painter: "Painter, we should like to have a house and furnish it." He said: "You must have one of two things—a comfortable house or a beautiful house. You can't have both. It is for you to choose." They said very meekly: "We are poets. We suppose we ought to think of a beautiful house." The painter replied: "In that case, nothing must enter the house for pleasure or comfort." They agreed. It was nine months before they had a chair. I have sat on the floor myself! If we are trying to furnish our soul, everything must be challenged—with a smile. I think possibly those poets had one of the simplest and most beautiful houses I ever saw, with a kind of stern poetic asceticism.

I think that Confession gives us the ascetic attitude towards the furnishing of our soul. When I think of the wisdom that has been shown to me in Confession since my seventh year, I am astonished at the munificence of God.

The unutterable consolation to me of this incident is that it took place in the house of Peter by the lakeside at Capharnaum. There, for the first time, man heard God call him "Son." That is accurate theology. When God has forgiven sin, the soul becomes again the child of God. And it is on that note I should just like to end. I would like to leave you with Our Lord saying to you and me: "Son, thy sins are forgiven thee." It might well touch our heart and our eyes to tears. Those words mean the intimate communion of the soul with our Redeemer. Now He stands and knocks, as if He had nothing to give, but something to receive. We do give Him something, but is something so unutterably beneath our receiving. The only thing we can really offer Him is what He has given us. We can only offer Him something back. We offer Him what we have received—a receiving of His Precious Blood; and an invitation to come and sit down by His side, from the lower seats at the table. He gives us the place of honour, not as guests, but as His sons. When we return to God, in Confession, we become His sons again, and He gives a most glorious banquet for the wedding of His Son.

"Go into thy own house." That means some external possession; "quies in termino"; rest in our home. "MY Church"; it is my Church; my house. When Heaven is given to me, it is mine; my house and my home. "MY God." We call Him that in such an intimate way, as if He were no other person's God.

We have Confession. Nothing here below is of greater importance. It is the obverse of the perfect union of the soul with God in Holy Communion. I am not sure that Holy Communion would work its fruits in our soul if we were not prepared for it by the Sacrament of Penance. Millions go to Confession that need not. They have the instinct that it is the best preparation for the intimacies of internal communion of the soul with its Eucharistic Redeemer.

May we, then, think of this exquisite scene as an intimacy of the revelation of God's Mercy to our poor God-thirsty soul. We want to be alone with some of these phrases. I want to be alone with "Lying on a bed." I just feel like that palsied one. I feel the graciousness of those bearing me along. I have no sense of being alone. I am in the company of others—borne by others so gracious as to say I am bearing them, when I know they are bearing me.

God grant us, then, to arise, and to take up the outward symbol of our weakness, and to enter into the great home which is made for us by the unutterable Mercy of God.

(*God's Way of Mercy*)

FORGIVENESS AFTER FALLS

Mark 14:29,30. But Peter saith to Him: Although all shall be scandalised in Thee, yet not I.

And Jesus saith to him: Amen I say to thee, today, even in this night, before the cock crow twice, thou shalt deny Me thrice.

No CHARACTER in the New Testament is quite so consoling and challenging as St. Peter—none. And we should all have a personal devotion to him, who was the mouthpiece of the human race when he acknowledged he was a sinner. Jesus couldn't redeem the world from sin until the world knew its sin and said: "I am a sinner"; so Peter that morning was the mouthpiece of the whole world.

Now there was that glorious profession of his humility; but what is very reassuring to us, dear children in Jesus Christ, is that he continued to be a sinner. He did not turn at once from all the weakness of his soul. Although he had courage to leave everything behind to follow Jesus, that did not mean perfection to him. He was still headstrong and wayward, weakness masquerading as strength and impulsiveness which called itself courage; some standing habits that had to be carefully uprooted one by one.

Are we not describing ourselves? Indeed, when we read the terrible account of St. Peter cursing and swearing that he did not even know Our Lord, you and I are inclined to think that we are very bad, but we've never quite done that; and even if we had, not after the special privileges given to St. Peter.

It was, of course, a sin of passion, wrung from him mostly by fear; but wasn't it a terrible thing that a man accustomed to such dangers as he had been, on some storm-ridden lake, should be overcome with fear?

We, by the Grace of God, often get spells of fervour and light, when we see things; we see God and we see ourselves; we see the sinfulness of ourselves, and we are amazed that, after the extraordinary graces God has given us, we are quite ordinary. Our desires are largely bounded by purely earthly things.

Of course you, dear children in Jesus Christ, by the Mercy of God and the hospitality of the dear sisters here, have had an opportunity of spending a little time in an atmosphere entirely aloof from the world. That is a very great grace. The very noises of this great city have hardly penetrated. It is an atmosphere of eternal ideas, fundamental principles of the human soul and even human society. You have been thinking far more deeply than the statesmen who are trying—I think vainly—to prevent civilisation from running on the rocks.

That is a very great thing. God has not just been niggardly. He has given not merely light but strength to take steps—even perseverance. Don't be too much humiliated that your steps today seem hardly as strong as your steps of twenty years ago. Years may have increased many of the difficulties; it may argue no enfeebling of your spiritual power. The first of all the virtues is perseverance.

We have in this figure of St. Peter one who saw the light, and was given strength, and then fell again. This is really the deepest subject of encouragement. We know what St. Peter became, a glorious martyr—such a glorious official martyr that Jesus spoke of his death as of His own self in His death—that it would be to the glory of God—as our death may one day be to the glory of God. One day we may put an end to our weakness and to our sin, and, if not in the last years, even our last deliberate action may yet be to the glory of God.

But I think these last words in St. Mark's Gospel about St. Peter are almost of the greatest reassurance, "And immediately the cock crew again. And Peter remembered the word that Jesus had said unto him . . . and he began to weep." They give you a new Peter, not just a reed chastened, hardened into a rock, but a rock which had been softened, powdered, dissolves. No doubt those that saw, possibly for the first time, the tears of Peter, wondered how the rough fisherman could be so unmanly as to shed tears. They might have imagined that he was losing his natural strength of character; the fact is he was beginning to have supernatural strength; he was just beginning to build up God's Kingdom in his soul almost on the ruins of his nature.

But, of course, dear children, God creates no ruins in the human soul. God will sometimes pull up the foundations, if they are built on sand. But God has no ruins. He preserves, and adds as much to the nature of a man as the oak adds to the nature of an acorn. Now we have the consolation of seeing Peter weeping at remembering some word of Jesus Christ. When Our Lord spoke those words, they may almost have irritated St. Peter and made him begin his disgraceful craft of cursing—when Jesus told him to his face that he would curse. But now those words come back again, and back again with some strange power. He had no joy in remembering. And yet, of course, the memory of One he really loved had something of joy in it, and in these words was the music of consolation that set the sinner on the great way of weeping.

There are saints of God like St. Joseph, a few like that, preserved from any great sin, and Our Dear Lady absolutely sinless; they have that consolation. But they belong so officially to the Incarnation itself, they are not so much our model as this model in sinful clay, that somehow or other before it died could chant what Our Lady could never say, *"Felix culpa."* Our Lady could never say, "Lord, be merciful to me, a sinner." And is there anything we desire to say more than that?—with something like peace in our soul—hope, gratitude, a sort of daily gratitude, making us even thankful we have sinned, for otherwise we should never have reached the possibility of being forgiven.

Peter's tears—and all are recorded—are great official tears—as the tears of His Master are recorded as being very, very official and redemptive.

There was just one thing necessary for that official sinner to complete his official office and represent you and me—the tears of Peter; tears of most bitter humiliation, terrible almost; tears of fierce anger against himself, for that a little serving-maid and a few serving-men had made him curse and swear that he did not know the Beloved of his heart.

But oh! my Beloved Saviour, Peter's oaths seem to bring him nearer to Thee than before. Before his denial there were many hard words for Peter; after this, none. Thou wert all sweetness, as if the only way to Thy Heart was by cursing and swearing that we do not know Thee —turning our back on Thee.

All these glorious memories are in the great heart of

Peter, as with something of sweet-bitterness of heart, he tells of the doings of that awful night. Judas is in that night; but hardly so deep in his crime as this Apostle who swore he did not know his Lord.

Yet, from all of it, in every word, comes the music of Peter's uprising. He suddenly blossomed into a most perfect and never recalled repentance.

Is there anyone, therefore, nearer to us inside the Gospel pages or outside the Gospel pages? This was written for our instruction, for our encouragement, for our example. And so, as we have all got St. Peter's way of waywardness and weakness and ten thousand defeats, let us begin St. Peter's way of weeping, sorrow and repentance. When we look back on our poor life, it must be with sweet-bitterness of soul; sweet because we cannot fail to see the mercy of God, and, seeing that mercy and pardon, we can turn our eyes with hope to the future. Had I only myself, I should be bowed down with despair; but when I see the mercy of God, I rise to hope. And to such transcendent hope that I feel almost gratitude, not for my sin, but for the occasion my sins have been to me to mistrust myself and to cast my care upon God.

Some day you will read St. Peter's Epistle. There you will find him asking you to cast your care upon God, because He careth for you. Peter remembered that, even in the night when he denied that he knew God, God did not deny that He knew Peter. God was by his side, shepherding him. God had a care of Peter. So we must all cast our care upon Him who ever has a care of us. And whatever danger now affrights us, dangers of life or death, we shall just leave to the care of Him who has care of us. He has greater care of us than ever we have for ourselves; greater love for us than we have for ourselves. May Jesus Christ, at the intercession of St. Peter, give us to reap the fruits of hope and comfort that may well be reaped from these memories of Peter's repentant tears.

(*God's Way of Mercy*)

LAST LETTER TO HIS BROTHER PATRICK

St. Dominic's Priory
Southampton Rd.
London, S.W.5
14—Apl.—1943

My dearest brother
            Deo gratias
This is the first time in my life that my letter to you has
begun with "Thanks be to God"—because it is the first
time in my life when I can tell you that God is asking my
life.

Only to-day have the doctors told me, what I knew
they would tell me that I have a malignant growth in
the throat. I presume my death is now only a matter of
a few weeks at most.

After having suffered the fears of death for a long lifetime, I thank God that He has taken the fears away.

I have a kind of joy or peace as if after a hard day's
work on one's feet it was time to lie down and rest.

You will be much in my thoughts and prayers. Keep
me in yours.

Good-bye and au revoir in heaven.

Your loving brother in
    J · M · J · D
        Fr. Vincent Joseph, O.P.

PRAYER OF FATHER VINCENT

O God, the Maker and Master of my being,
I adore Thee from the heights and depths of my soul.
Of Thy great love, Thou hast brought me forth from nothing;
and unto nothing should I come, if Thou didst withdraw
    Thy hand of love.
What shall I give Thee, what dost Thou ask in return
    for such love?
If Thou dost ask my time, I will give Thee all my days;
If Thou dost ask my mind, I will give Thee all my thoughts;
If Thou dost ask my love, I will give Thee all my heart,
to be Thine without recall now and for evermore.
        AMEN.

ACKNOWLEDGMENTS

Blackfriars Publications (London) and Newman Press (Westminster, Md.): "The Scruple of Doubt," and "Hindrances to Prayer," both from *Faith and Prayer* (1953).

The Editor of *Blackfriars* (Oxford): "A Chair of the Philosophy of History" (vol. 12); "Gilbert Keith Chesterton" (vol. 17); "Canticum Magorum" (vol. 6); "Follow Me" (vol. 9); "Non Nisi Te, Domine" (vol. 9); "Rosa Patientiae" (vol. 13); and "St. Thomas" (vol. 5).

Burns Oates & Washbourne (London): "Nazareth Measures," "Rights of the Parent," "To the Child in the Manger," "The Two Kings," "A Tale of Two Cities," and "A Call to Contemplatives," from *The Church and the Land* (1926); "The Problem of Suffering," "The Joy of Suffering," and "The Tears of Jesus," from *The Craft of Suffering* (1936); "The Mercy of God," "Good Tidings," "Confession," and "Forgiveness after Falls," from *God's Way of Mercy* (1938); "The Place of Fear," "The Passing of Children's Games," "The Home of Song," and "The Creator Child," from *The Wayside* (1934).

The Catholic Truth Society (London): *Confession to a Priest* (complete; 1941).

Ditchling Press (Ditchling, England): "Francis Thompson," from *Francis Thompson & Other Essays* (1936).

P. J. Kenedy & Sons (New York): "St. Dominic," from *From a Friar's Cell* (1924).

The Editor of *Life of the Spirit* (Rugeley, England): Eulogy by Hilary Carpenter, O.P. (vol. 7).

The Macmillan Company (New York): "The Children's Catechism," from *The Catholic Church and Philosophy* (1927).

Mr. Patrick McNabb (Melrose, Mass.): Last Letter to His Brother, and "Prayer of Father Vincent."

The Newman Press (Westminster, Md.): "Morning Prayer," "Perseverance in Prayer," and "Prayer—How Easy It Is," from *The Craft of Prayer* (1951).